Order of Appearance

Author's Note

There is a goodness inside us. Sometimes we nurture this and help it grow, sometimes we poison our goodness with thoughts of what we lack. By blaming anyone but ourselves for our happiness, by allowing ourselves to have "only if" thoughts, or by asking of the Universe that which we are not willing to do for others, we create imbalance in our lives.

Your peace is none of my business. What brings you joy cannot be my concern. It is not for me to determine the fairness of the way the Divine has treated you. What I can offer you is this. The beginning of contentment, the start of abundance, the feeling of satisfaction at the end of the day, is generated by a simple gratitude at the start of the day.

My sister said once that others accuse her of seeing things through "rose colored" glasses, because she was optimistic and held higher hopes for relationships than most. My response was,

"Little sister... perhaps they are just looking at the world through "poo-colored" glasses".

Be the wonderful you, you are. Smile at times that find others frowning. Enjoy the ability to see the present moment both for what it is, and also for what joy it might help to bring. But above anything else, give thanks. Gratitude is what brings more goodness. And as a note of advice, tell people why you are thankful for them, but keep other things you are thankful for between you and God.

Introduction

Most people have struggled, at one time, or another, to be better. To feel better. To act in a way that considers something other than themselves. Consider what follows as an encouragement to do this. Consider what follows as, perhaps a way, to get to that point in living where there is progress. Please do not consider these words as a criticism. What is in this book should be uplifting. It should be an indulgence, a chance to consider things normally not thought about during the course of a regular day, and it should, with every story, make you proud of who you are.

When we decide to do a thing. When we have a thought or inclination that our lives may be for more than just consuming time and goods or working to be able to do those two things, there is a tendency for ourselves and others to judge us, based on our aspirations or goals. My mother used to say, when one of us would offer information about a family situation that might prove embarrassing, "You don't have to tell everything you know".

This is true of a lot of things, and especially your goals with the Creator. Your dreams might be shared, but if you share them with someone who is not invested in making them come true, it diminishes the power of the dream dramatically. Even something as simple as saying to someone, "I think I will lose ten pounds", will decrease the drive, determination, and the ability to lose ten pounds. Share secrets with the Universe. Be at peace knowing that the Universe, or God, or The Divine, or whatever you choose to call that Source, has everything you need. Be certain that those you are compelled to speak your dreams to, do not. This is not to diminish the help or concern of others, but it is to create a bond or relationship with you and the One who created everything.

These writings are mostly thoughts that have occurred to me over the last two years. They are a collection of stories and ideas that might be inconsistent. They are a collection of suggestions, mainly to my future self, that are best enjoyed by a reader who wishes to think about possibilities rather than develop a belief system. Some ideas may contradict each other. Some ideas might be contrary to what you already believe. Some ideas, even still, might be directly opposed to what I claim to believe. This is alright with me. The purpose of these stories is to find you where you are, express a deep appreciation for the person you are, and challenge you to find ways to create kindness in the world. Seems simple enough.

Just a word before the sharing of my world starts. We, as humans, do not have to know everything. We do, however, have to know we do not know everything. We, as participants in the world of the Creator, but we do have to know ours is not the only world of the Creator. We should have needs, wants, and desires, but we should never assume we know those things for another. What I hope you find in this collection is some word, phrase, or story, that helps you where you are. For me, it is in the telling of stories that I find solace. For me, a story helps me recall things that help me in other situations. My favorite times are sitting and listening to accounts of what is important to people at any age.

At the end of this book, there will be a website listed. It is a shameless advertisement for a project that my eleven-year old son and I have started which will help homeless and lower income folks generate cash. Please, if you do nothing else, take the time to use the "contact us" icon on that website to share your stories with me. That is, if you think I am trustworthy enough, to hold them in my thoughts. I trust that you will use these stories in a positive way, to improve your life. If you are tempted to use them to improve someone else's life, please share the book, but please share in a positive, encouraging, way.

If you wonder who to be, just be. If you wonder what to be, just be. If you wonder how to be, just be. You, with all your faults, and all your unclaimed virtues, are a miracle. Treat yourself that way. Afford yourself grace when it is needed. Remind yourself of the present when you are tempted to be shamed by your past or anxious about your future. Take care of a plant, a pet, a friend, or stranger, when you think the world has conspired against you. And at the very least, say "thank you" for something, every day. My belief is that you are better than you know.

Lessons from Children

Children know things. They have ideas. Some seem foolish to our adult minds, while some may remind us of truths we might have forgotten. Sometimes we hear a thought a child thinks, and we dismiss it quickly. Sometimes we encourage a child to pursue that thought and build it into a theory. Just as I would never take the advice of a teacher, a text, or a tradition as fact, without thought and consideration, I do not take the words of a child as truth simply because they are spoken from a newer place in life's experience, but if I had to pick between the advice of a child, or a televangelist, the child wins every time.

Lesson 1: *From Whence We Came*

My nephew, when he was three, bounced up and down, up and down, up and down, on my mother's bed. My mother was trying to take a nap and could not, because there was a toddler playing trampoline next to her. When I asked my nephew what in the world he was doing, he looked at me, smiled giggled a little and said with some measure of excitement, "I was born before I was born".

I had been reading some thought on reincarnation. I had often wondered about the afterlife and how we "got here" in this world. Here was my nephew, excited, looking me straight in the eye while smiling, and exclaiming, "I was born before I was born".

I still have no opinion on reincarnation. I cannot say with certainty what the afterlife will be. My suspicion is there is no after life. My suspicion is there is a continued life. And while we may have been born forty times into this world, it matters very little, to the work we have to do here now. But his smile and confidence has stuck with me. I was, indeed, born before I was born. We all were. Do you think I was born yesterday? Yes. I was. And the day before that, and the day before that. We are always new. We are always beginners. We are reborn every day.

Lesson 2: *The Red Bird*

My son Carter came to us when he was five years old. Six or seven years later, he deals with family dynamics that are different, at least, and perhaps more difficult, than some other kids his age. On a positive note, at least there are family dynamics for him to figure out. It could be worse, but that observation never helped anyone going through any trial or trouble. Carter new my mother for a few years before her passing, as "Grandmamma". They loved each other.

After a particularly rough situation was temporarily resolved with regard to Carter's holiday schedule, I was a bit concerned for Carter's mental state when I left for work recently. He is tough. He can handle anything. I was just concerned that he might get caught up in the daily situation and not focus on the "bigger picture things" that tell us we are going to make it through whatever happens to come upon us. We teach that sort of thing in our house.

I came home tired. I put my things away. I fell into the couch beside Carter and said, "How was your day".

Carter smiled and said, "I saw Grandmamma".

"Oh yeah?", I replied… "How was she?".

He explained that he looked out a window and there was a red bird calling and that he understood Grandmamma to say, "Everything is going to be okay".

We did not have a conversation on symbolism. We did not determine in our minds whether that was an embodiment of my mother or my actual mother. We did not wonder if my mother had sent the bird, or if it was the Creator, or if it was of the red bird's own volition that Carter had seen it. Grandmamma told him it was going to be okay. That is really all I needed to hear. And really, that is all Carter needed to hear. And to be honest, my lesson had nothing to do with messages from the beyond. It was that everything, is indeed, going to be okay.

Lesson 3: *The Pants*

When I was growing up, my parents made some questionable decisions. Well… really only one that I know about for certain. The pants. If I wore today, what they proudly adorned me with in the 1970's, I would be ridiculed. Plain and simple.

I do not know if I looked good then. I do not know if that was the style. What I do know, is that I do not remember one pair of those pants from memory. I do not remember if there was a dress code, or how much my outfits cost, or if I was cool because I buttoned my top button or chose to wear the neckline low. Thank the heavens above, my childhood memories have little to do with what I wore or what I looked like.

The thing for me to remember, the lesson I learned from the child I was, is that the pants I have on now, might be as odd in thirty years, as the busy little numbers I wore to elementary school. What somebody else is wearing, or how they look, will not matter at all, and should not matter, at all. Great tools to express themselves, but not a great help for seeing the person behind the wardrobe. My lesson, see people, hear people, understand people. You do not have to help everyone you see, but why not make it a goal? The child we know best is the child we were.

At My Age

I am nearly fifty years old. I am convinced that my continued education in matters of life should be split between learning new things and unlearning things I believe to be true. There is truth in the world, but it is so hard to get to the core of what is true. I do not believe there is "my truth" and "your truth" and "the truth of the guy across the world". There are realities that are different, but truths are cheapened if we do not take the time to find the universality of what is true for everyone.

As adults, innocently enough, in our quest for truth, we want to ask everyone to "prove" it. I always found it humorous that founders of religions are recorded to have said so little in comparison with the volumes of words used to somehow expand on what a leader or founder of a religion has said. It is staggering. Buddha, Jesus, Mohamed, Zarathustra, Moses, all of the Rishis in all of Hinduism, and even their disciples, have so few words. We blame our charity and our wars on these people. And we sell our opinions of them like we sell used cars.

So, yes, I have much to unlearn. I did not learn most of what I "know" on purpose. Somethings I need to unlearn I have yet to discover about myself. But what I do not ask of children teachers, is proof. Children are closer to the source of God than I have been in fifty years. We are from God. We tend to forget that. God is closer to us than our next heartbeat. We tend to forget that also. And as for you? What truth is there that I know for you?

You have choices. You have a story. You have something to teach and you have something to learn. When you think about giving up, the balance between what you think of yourself and how the Divine sees you is out of balance. When you think about giving up, you may need help. We all need help at times. On the good days, you are the help for someone else. You are an eternal being in a temporary situation. To paraphrase Dr. Wayne Dyer, "you are a spiritual being having a human experience, not a human having spiritual experiences".

My Advice

Be you. Enjoy you. If you do not enjoy you, change you. And share your joy.

Did You Say Peace?

Sometimes I feel like we have given up on the notion of peace. On Christmas, it seems appropriate to ponder such a thing. At times, there is this notion that peace means weakness. That peace is a giving up on individuality. That the cost of peace is conformity. What I do know, is that peace is not possible for the whole earth, but peace, is very possible, on earth.

I believe the song went like this. "Peace on earth, goodwill to men". Do these two things go hand in hand? Most likely. The Teacher said it with some authority and advised that before prayer, if you have anything which is not peace with your brother or sister, you should handle the situation with others before you approach the throne of God.

I do not know how this could be simpler, or more
direct.

This notion of the light of our mind. Whether
those we have an issue with are here, deceased, in
another country, or just down the street, we can
offer forgiveness and love by surrounding them
with light in our minds. Is this a physical light? No.
Does this affect them immediately? No. What it
does, is give us a way to change our reaction to the
thought of them, which, in turn, will change the way
we react to them. Or even just the thought (in the
case of the parted or distant) of them. We can wish
them well, wish them health, wish for them the
things we would like for ourselves, but from a place
of peace.

This notion of giving beyond reason. When a
person does a thing that directly affects us, the only
thing we can change is our reaction. Honestly, some
people are just on a different level of consciousness
than we would prefer. For some, the only person in
their world is that person. Which is fine. Use these
people for what they can be used for. Not our ability

to change others, but our ability to react with love.
When someone gives you the finger in traffic a mile
down the road, offer to let them in your lane when
they need to change lanes. When someone snubs
you at work, go out of your way to speak well of
them to a coworker. When a spouse (not mine, ever,
of course) presents a request that seems
unreasonable to you, fulfill that request while
smiling and end the task with a kiss and smile.

This notion of a butterfly. There is a theory
that the flap of the butterfly's wing might cause a
tsunami on the other side of the world by the events
it sets in motion. It is a neat theory. But what if it
does not. What if it is, just a butterfly. That is fine,
too. Your peaceful actions, your random acts of
kindness, your wishing well for others may not
change the world. It will change your world.
Sometimes, speaking of the potential for changing
the life of another with a simple smile, is as
coercive an action as the threat of an eternity in hell
if we do ill towards others. When we let kindness be
kindness alone, we may not change the world, but

we will change our worlds. And peace "on earth"
does not mean peace "in all the earth".

This Christmas, and in the coming days, my
wish is peace. Perhaps not through peace treaties.
Perhaps not through laying down of arms. Perhaps,
though, through simple, intentional kindnesses, both
given and received. There will be rounds of
choruses this day exclaiming, "Peace to you". In
return there will be rounds of choruses this day
exclaiming, "And also to you". We cannot create
peace for the world. If we could, it would have been
done before now. We can, however, create peace
for ourselves. We do it with every breath, every
thought, and every step. And in doing so, we will
become beacons of peace for others to see, like a
lighthouse in dark night's storm. Not guiding a ship,
not changing its course, but by providing a
reference for only the sake of those sailing.

Love 101

"The beginning of love is the will to let
those we love be perfectly themselves, the

resolution not to twist them to fit our own image. If in loving them we do not love what they are, but only their potential likeness to ourselves, then we do not love them: we only love the reflection of ourselves we find in them." – Thomas Merton

Additionally, I might say, that the beginning of love is not the end. Love is eternal. Love is infinite. Love will endure when other things fade. At times, we may act in the name of love, but do deeds that serve only our desire to be needed. The best love is the love between the Creator and Its creation, that is kept a secret between them both.

If you are reading this essay, there is a good chance that you have been born into this world. Most likely, you have had times you describe as troublesome, and also times that you describe as good. And if you have been born into the world, have experienced any life at all, you will know "opposites". You will know gain and loss, joy and mourning, greed and charity, happiness and despair.

The Divine, being perfectly Itself, is constantly giving good things. Wants for us, abundance. Not in order for us to have much, but to recreate Its work of giving good things in the world. The Divine is a healer, who is always making healing available to those needing to be healed. In the words of the gospel singers, "God is a way maker", always helping those in tune with divine intuition to do great things with seemingly few resources.

And about us humans? We diminish God when we pray prayers of request or ask God to give us a thing, or to heal a friend, or to make a way. It is as if we are a five-year old child, while watching his or her mother make a birthday cake, remind the baker to use the correct mixer while creating the batter. It is as if, while watching Babe Ruth walk up to bat, we remind him that the objective is to hit a home run. When we approach the throne of God with a desire, we are assuming the Divine has abundance, but for some reason is keeping abundance from us.

God made you in God's image. Worry not for being more God like. There is no way of knowing with certainty what God is like (and anyway, that is a lot of pressure). Participate in the work of God, as best you know how, and love others in a way that makes them think of God, rather than you. Do not limit God or suggest ways God might provide for the world, your loved ones, or you. Assume the Universe is desperately trying to give everyone alive today, the abundance, joy, and peace they desire.

Be grateful, expect good things, be grateful, accept good things, be grateful, share. Repeat.

It really is this simple. Our petition is not what we offer on our knees, but what is made known in how we treat others. Our devotion is not voiced with fancy words, but with what we share with others. Our worth is not determined by the things we have, but in remembering we, and everyone around us, are from and will return, to the Divine.

If you need a religion to remind you of this, please join a religion. If you need to let a charity, in exchange for your money, do charitable works on your behalf, by all means, give to a charity. If you need a teacher to make this clearer, sit under a teacher. If it helps to meditate, pray, or breathe deeply, then do these things with frequency. Love does not require any of these, though some may find them necessary.

Your heart just beat again. You drew another breath. Enjoy. You must have more to accomplish. There must be at least one more good thing for you to enjoy. Be at peace and know that you are a both a product, and a creator, of love.

Positive, Well Meaning, Thought

Typically, I do not hide the fact that I work for a large, express tunnel, car wash company on social media. And again, typically, I do not hide the fact from my employer, that I write blogs on topics other than washing cars. Sometimes, these ventures are similar, but they never clash. Fortunately, the values that I strive to promote are the same values found in the company I am helping to build. I hope that my character is consistent, regardless of the proverbial "hat" I am wearing on any given day.

Car washing, and the layout of the wash where I began my car washing career, made it easy to preconceive a thought about a customer before meeting them. Before the first word is spoken, you know what kind of car they drive, how they are dressed, by virtue of parking stickers, where they work, and what they were willing to spend to keep their car clean. There is no intuition required. It is not a market strategy or an effort to collect customer data, it is just information presented and received. Early on, I began doing something for each person I met through my job.

A positive, intentional, well-meaning, thought. Every customer. Every time. No matter what I thought I might know about someone, or whether they deserved it, a positive, intentional, well-meaning, thought. It cost me nothing. The individual attention I had to give a customer when guiding them onto the track of the car wash afforded the opportunity. Nothing they would know about. Nothing I got paid extra to do.

It helped diffuse situations that involved customer concerns. It gave me the inclination to actively listen to their stories after they made it through the tunnel. It created friendships, that to this day, mean a great deal to me. Positive, intentional, well-meaning thought created an atmosphere where customers felt welcome somehow, without really knowing why.

These days, my time is shared with my old site and others in the area. The company I currently work with bought this wash and others over two years ago. When I return, I always see someone I know. We always catch up like we went to high school together so many years ago. We know each other's stories. We enjoy seeing each other again.

Some people say, "get to know your customer", as if it were like reading them in a poker game, or "find their spending habits", or (frightening) "track what apps they download on social media". There is no secret to engaging with customers, but it is fast becoming a lost art. Read their mood, but in an effort to know how they are feeling. Find their spending habits, but in order to make sure they are buying what they need, verses what you want them to purchase. Look at the apps on their phone, but because they used those apps to show you pictures of their kids, grand kids, or vacations.

You may never meet a sales goal for the month with this practice. It may never win you great recognition from a magazine or chamber of commerce. There will be no immediate monetary reward for your efforts. But it will sustain your business in lean times. It will allow you honest feedback when you are in need of information. And when you return to a site after a year of having not been there 45 hours a week, it will bring you and your customers joy.

Joy is a commodity that, though not traded on Wall Street, is as valuable as anything sold.

This is not rocket science. If it were, we would have never made it to the moon. Is it too mushy for the business world? Perhaps. Does it belong on a LinkedIn article? Maybe not. Businesses that offer a quality service, at a fair price, will thrive. Businesses that truly know their customers, will thrive more. We cannot know a customer until *we actually know* a customer. Without a positive, intentional, well-meaning thought, we have no right to even begin to know our customers.

Shine

It has been said that there are more ways than one to do a thing correctly. More than one way to do the right thing. Even if the choices of what to do are narrowed down to one, there is more than one way to accomplish a goal. As to how many ways, I would add, the Creator of the universe, as diverse as it is, expects this from a world that was created with so many different colors, organisms, life forms, and yes, personalities.

If we can accept that there are differences in the way our neighbors and ourselves do the right thing, how then are we to determine what is the right thing? My suggestion is to boil it down to this. Love one another. It is an admonition from several religions that goes unheeded, and worse even still, is practiced with no real understanding. Loving one another is not tolerating one another. Loving one another is not letting others be free to be themselves and alone. Loving one another, contrary to some religious thought, is not converting others to conform to a certain belief system.

Love is where you spend your time. Love is how you treat a person you have just met. Love is how you have treated someone that you have known for years. Love is giving gifts for no reason or helping when a person is in need. Love can be a prayer, a concern, or even a thought, but never in a condescending or manipulative way. Love is spreading around the love you have received from others and from God. It helps others and also makes room for more love to be received for yourself. It's sort of neat that way.

To love another, you must be in love. Not with "the other", but with something beyond yourself. Someone, or something, that loves you. And here is the thing about creation. You are loved. You are uniquely able to receive the love of the Creator. You cannot receive it like another, and you cannot receive it in its entirety, but the love that is for you is the same as others that are loved in their unique way. One love, many faces. One love, many hearts. One love, many traveled roads. So be in love. Keep it simple. Start small. And shine.

Never Let Them See You Sweat

In college, I heard of Columbia Baptist, in Falls Church, VA, located just outside of Washington DC. Turns out, they were looking for interns to work with children and youth. Housing, food, and a small stipend were offered. I interviewed and got the position. I spent three summers working for this church. Two as an intern, and one as the interim high school youth minister. The last summer provided more opportunity to program lessons and work with parents and leaders in the church.

If you have ever been provided with the opportunity to work more with parents and leaders in a church, you know it tends to kill the original enthusiasm you had for working with youth and children. The summer was filled with work that was just boring at times and not supported well by more than a few great people in the church. Being who I was, I said little to the parents and leaders of the church about my concerns.

Until the end of the summer. It was a custom of the church to celebrate the summer program with a special evening service where youth and the youth minister spoke about the program. There was large congregation and a big percentage of them showed up. My direct supervisor even borrowed a suit for me to wear. Being who I was, I declined to wear it. I invited some of the former interns up from my summers there, and we enjoyed seeing each other before my "talk".

I said, among other things (the passing of time warrants the paraphrasing), "I left home to come here and work this summer for housing, food, and a small stipend. I helped run a program for the summer without an education to do so, without a single parent volunteer, and while missing my home. My advice is that as soon as it is possible, you hire a fulltime youth minister to fill the vacant position."

I felt like a patch when a new tire was needed. I felt like a last-minute decision in a scramble to avoid paying a fulltime minister. I felt, for some reasons, there was little support from those who asked me to return again. In fairness, these were just my twenty-year old perceptions, and in fairness, my times at that church, in hindsight were some of the best days of my life. But there I was, standing in front of a large group of congregants, having said what I had said, with nothing to do but return to the pew before me. So, I did.

The pastor rose, situated himself behind the pulpit, looked me square in the eyes, and said,

"There's a saying in Christian ministry. Never let them see you sweat".

I interrupted what he thought would be a dramatic pause and said with a voice loud enough to reach the same people he had reached with the help of a microphone, "I think it is all part of being honest".

After some words, he instructed the congregation to hold someone's hand and pray. He came down and sat next to me, grabbed my hands and prayed what seemed to be more of an instruction to me than a petition to God. He literally grabbed my arm and led me to the back of the church, where it is customary for participants in the service to shake hands with the clergy as they exit. I shook hands with everyone and smiled a sly grin as if to say, "I think I struck a nerve", or "What just happened?".

Some years passed and I thought of that Sunday night. Whatever I did, good or bad, I made people think. But I also had unfinished business with that preacher. I tracked him down in a nursing home and called him and apologized for doing things the way I did and checked on him from time to time. We exchanged emails. I have since, again, lost track of him and my guess is that he has passed after caring for those people in the home where he spent his final years.

The meaning for me has nothing to do with honesty or letting people "see you sweat". It has nothing to do with whether you should have to wear a suit to speak to people about the Divine. And it certainly has nothing to do with righting wrongs before those you have offended pass quietly away in a nursing home. But there is still yet meaning for me in this story.

The passing of time makes me question the importance of the things I felt passionately about earlier in life. My later years leave me missing the good things about my past more so than wanting to complain about what I felt was troublesome. My perspective has changed, not because I am wiser, but because by choosing to be thankful for what was good rather than blame my present condition on the bad (and there have been some tough times), there is created in an intrigue and an instinct to wonder how present events will be later counted as gratitude.

Do we smile because we feel good, or do we feel good because we smile? Do good things happen because we help create them or do good things happen because they are a gift? We know so little about life, and the love and protection we receive every day. I am more hesitant to dismiss a person, or criticize an event these days, and I believe that matters. I suspect that whether we curse the thorns or bless the flower, neither will change the rose, but both will change our lives.

Billtown Road

Louisville, Kentucky never held a special place in my heart. When I was in high school, I visited a church there and worked on some building projects for about a week. Recently, I have been tasked with helping a site in this city as a part of what I do for a living. Today, while traveling to this part of the world, I heard a lyric from a Wyclef Jean song.

"Pouring sips of liquor out for my fallen squad" or something to that effect. My mind immediately went out to my friend Bill. A couple of years, or a year, or a lifetime ago, I'm not sure, I got word that Bill had passed. My mind took me to the roof of the Baptist Student Union at the University of Tennessee, where we smoked cigars drank non-alcoholic beer as we watched countless sunsets and talked about life. I thought it might be that I would smoke a cigar tonight in his honor. Then, as the miles passed, I grew increasingly angry.

One of the stories that I heard about Bill insinuated that he had killed himself. If you knew Bill, you know what a shock this story came to those hearing it for the first time. Bill was all the best that is in each of us. Bill and I smiled all the time back in our college days. There is probably a blog about him on this website. I was mad at Bill. And I cried while driving. In my mind, cussing him, and wondering where he got off taking such a life away from those who loved him.

Then I got a sense of peace as I remembered those who have passed after spending a time in my life. I thought of my mother, who loved Bill, and Bill's father, who died soon after Bill. I thought of them together, enjoying whatever the passing from this world brings. I forgave Bill, gave a silent pardon if you will. I spoke and said aloud, in a car alone, "It's cool, Dude".

At that moment, somewhere outside or just inside of Louisville, Kentucky, I saw an exit sign I had not seen in my recent trips. Billtown Rd. Bill nodded back, and said, "It's cool, Dude". Bill was a friend, that if you were lucky enough to have, you never doubted he was on your side. It has taken me some time to admit he pissed me off that day. But I think we are finally square. And for what it is worth, through whatever God has provided for such things, I still feel like he is on my side.

Life is both sad and happy at the same time. There are mysteries I do not understand and graces that I take for granted. When I think back on my times with an old friend, I feel like a teenager believing that life is simple. Black and white. That God is on the side of whatever group I choose to be a part of. Experience has taught me that God is bigger than what most choose to believe and that our brothers and sisters might very well be in groups we feel are in opposition to the Divine.

Do I really believe that this trip to Louisville held a message from a friend I have not seen in years? I do. Do I understand that this type of belief is unorthodox and might be considered insane? I do.

These days I enjoy listening to stories that people tell. I like hearing books on Audible. My days start with some music and light meditation and they end with a word of thanks. The middle part is full of finding order in what appears to be the chaos of living. That is what makes me happy.

You can have CNN and Fox news. You can have your Southern Baptist verses Catholic theological debates. You can have your 100,000-mile warranties and brighter, whiter, smiles. It all seems meaningless to me. If it is meaningful to others, more power to them. I miss the days that I had the time, and the opportunity, to hang out with Bill. And as crazy as it sounds, I feel like I got to do that again today in the short time it took to catch an interstate exit sign out of the corner of my eye.

My Catholic Friend

Though my life has been filled with respect for those in and of the Catholic faith, I have never been compelled to join the church. My journey has been filled with other groups and other belief systems. These groups and belief systems have always allowed me to revere Catholic thought and theology, but they, by being independent organizations, left little room for conversion. As a college student, I became enamored by Meister Eckhart's sermons. In my twenties, Thomas Merton fascinated me. In more recent years, I have grown to enjoy the life and words of Mother Teresa.

These figures seem to have been on the fringe of the church's teachings at times and admittedly, that is what drew me to them. They did little to affect my opinion of the church. They did little to drive me to the church. What has made me intrigued as of late by the Catholic church as a vehicle of God's love, is my experience with a life-long friend. I have known her for most of my life and she is a family friend. In my opinion, if there ever was an example of God's love, it would be who we will call for the sake of this story, "Susan".

Susan drives my thoughts to the Church and to God Himself. If you will indulge my storytelling, I will share the reasons why. In full disclosure, Susan does not know I am writing this article. Susan may not even know how I feel about my experience of her. And in full disclosure, my suspicion is that many more people have experienced this love of life and God that lives in Susan than only me. While I may not do the story justice, the story I will share, all with the intention of conveying how well she has represented Catholicism and God.

Compassion

When my mother was diagnosed with angiosarcoma, it came as a shock to my family. More shocking than the diagnosis, was the life expectancy of those with the diagnosis. My mother, though not bed-ridden or house bound, spent the last years of her life on the phone, spreading the love of God and providing a listening ear to her friends and family. She wrote letters and filled out cards, she kept a prayer journal, and she was a joy to those who knew her. Susan had known her for over forty years, but I am unsure how much they kept in contact. I was instructed from time to time by both my mother and Susan to pass messages of "Hello" and "Thinking of you" to one another. One day I walked into my mother's house, after it was apparent her physical death was near, to find a beautiful bouquet of flowers near the television.

The obvious question for me to ask was, "Who sent you flowers?".

Her answer was simple, and she said with a smile, "Susan brought them by".

Susan brought flowers from her church to my mother. It meant the world to my mother, not only that the flowers were beautiful, but that they had been a part of a church service. My mother was a life-long Southern Baptist and Susan was a devout Catholic. As important as religion was to each of them, people were more important. It was if they were winking at one another and saying, "Our races are almost run. We will meet again. There is something more than either of us know that will bring us together again."

As it turns out, this was not quite the end for my mother. She still had a few weeks to live in her earthly form. There was one more gift for Susan to give. It gave my mother comfort and it made me imagine that there was more to God and the Catholic Church than I had ever dreamed. The gift was a blanket that Susan and her fellow parishioners prayed over and was to be used to console and as a request for healing for my mother. To this day, I am impressed with the practicality and the intent of this gift of love that Susan and the people of her church gave to my mother. It was then that I started noticing, not only the differences in our world's religions, but also the similarities. And while all religions may not be equal, these acts of compassion allowed me to see actions of compassion around me more and more.

Smiling

Quite frankly, there is no need for me to inform anyone in the Catholic church, that in the world apart from the Catholic church, there is an unease about how those in the church treat people. Often, these stories have more to do with the issues of those who have the negative opinion. I am guilty of this in my own perceptions of many organizations and individuals. With this admission, I would like to say that Susan changed my opinion of the Catholic church with one smile. Not that is was a bad opinion. Not that there was any hurt or ill will when I thought of the Church. Susan makes me proud of the Catholic church. And as much pressure as this seems to be, she represents all that is good with God to me.

After her husband passed away, the only thing I could do was hug her. After my mother died, a hug was all I needed from her. We do not speak in long sentences. We do not spend hours discussing this or that issue. We see each other every 2-3 weeks and we smile and hug. There is a knowing when we meet again, time after time. It is a knowing that there is a God and that He loves us, where we are, how we are, and that He has more in store for each of us. All of this with one smile. There are no issues with theology, politics, hot button topics, or any issues that need to be debated. Just smiles to be shared.

Pride, Humility, and Gratitude

Susan is proud of her church. She knows she is a small part of the Church. Every time I see Susan, I see that she is thankful for everything she has been given and had the chance to experience. Each time I speak to her, I am left wanting to know more about what makes her, her. Susan's quiet assurance and sweet spirit compel me to ask why I am so lucky to know, and be a part of, her family (though I had a wonderful mother, I have always considered myself adopted into her brood). On the days she is missed from our regular meetings, it is usually because there is a function at her church that she is helping with, and I know when I hear the reason for her absence, she is happy, and those around her are happy, as well. Susan is proud. Susan is, at the same time, humble. And in everything, she is grateful. While I am not proposing sainthood, I am venerating her spirit that embodies what I would want from anyone representing anything I thought was important.

From the Wilderness

In fairness, it should be stated that I was not far from, in my experience, the Catholic church. As the president of the Baptist Student Union at the University of Tennessee, I stepped next door many days to the Catholic Student Center to participate in Mass. While neither group captured my heart enough for me to participate as a regular member today, they shaped who I am today. This wilderness I speak of is really a matter of perception. What some might call a mission field, another might call home. What some might call a church, some might call a bowling alley. This is a big world and the Catholic church is a big church. There are many members and many opportunities for human, rather than Divine, influence.

As a non-Catholic, it behooves me to say to the Catholic church, "Keep up the good compassionate work of God".

There seems to be some fascination in the world with picking this or that flaw out of Catholicism and beating the issue to death and more. Though I am unsure what the good or pleasure there is in this type of reporting for those that report, I am sure there are more stories like the ones about Susan that are not reported. Always more good stories than bad stories. I used to be interested in Catholic/Southern Baptist dialogue. What I found was there was mostly discussion about theology and dogma and finding common ground based on ideology.

In my later years I have found, that the dialogue I am interested in does not simply leave me with a list of ideological things I might agree on with someone from another faith, or religion, or denomination, but a dialogue that leaves me with a shared appreciation of another *person* following a different path. And just like a review on social media, one bad apple might spoil the bunch, if those experiencing a person of a faith are susceptible to letting others affect their opinion of God. Though I do not know if one good apple can save the bunch, it might be better to at least notice good apples than worry for the bad ones. Susan is a good apple.

This chapter supposes to be about the Catholic church and admittedly is more about one member of that church. Is this not the Church? The people. Is this not the good stuff? I do not want to suggest that I know what God wants from anyone, but I do know what He has shown me, with the through, Susan. What I know of the Catholic church is influenced

by her. I admire her resolve to hold fast to faith. I
am envious of her dedication devotion to the
Church. Our lives have intersected at this point, in
time and space, and she is one of the reasons that I
know, beyond knowing, that there is a God and that
this God cares for everyone. And if I needed to
know anything other than these, I could not imagine
what it might be. As Jesus represented God, as the
apostles represented Jesus, and as all that followed
represented everyone that came before, Susan
represents the institution that is the Catholic church,
in a new, empathetic, compassionate way.

Do You Guru?

Why are gurus in high altitudes? Maybe the
air is better up there. Maybe it is closer to heaven
and the voice of God is heard more clearly in
relation to our ears' proximity to heaven. Richard
Branson might make yet another fortune teaching
meditation classes in "super high altitude"
classrooms soaring at 35,000 feet through the
atmosphere. Not, of course, because it would

provide a benefit, but because people, especially those searching for answers, are gullible.

Personally, I have never traveled to a mountain top to speak with a guru. In this day and age, there seems little need to travel around the world and then trek up a mountain to ask questions that Siri or Cortana can answer in an instant. Even in lower altitudes. Teachers that cloister themselves away offer no better a perspective, but a different perspective. Even so, especially now, people need the advice of those who do not have the trappings of worrying about a busy, materialistic, *"only more"* way of life. Here are some things that are important about gurus on the mountains.

It Is the Journey

What makes the wisdom of a mountain dweller seem wise, is that by the time a pilgrim or seeker makes their way to the mountain top, the pilgrim or seeker is more able to hear the words of a guru. This is why people are changed by speaking to those living apart from the valleys of the world. And while we tend to think only of the journey towards the top of the mountain filled with our questions as being of worth. The journey down the mountain, filled with our new perspective, and hopefully just as many, but different, questions is just as important.

Gurus at the Gas Station

Until we see every person we meet as a guru, able to teach us something on our way through life (even when we stop for gas), we will not be ready to learn from the very wise. Even the crabby attendant. Even the person that cut you off to take your "next" spot in line to get gasoline. Even the old man we see each and every time we buy a soda or fill up our tanks, that has, "a sick granddaughter that just got out of the emergency room and needs to get a prescription filled". We need to pick *who we learn from*, but we need to realize that *everyone can teach us*.

Someone Wants to Be You

I never found much solace in the notion that "some people don't even get to drive a car" when I was upset about having a flat tire on the interstate. I never was compelled to eat more Brussels Sprouts because another child in China did not have food that night. Life has taught me, however, that no matter what problems we create or imagine for ourselves, there is another person that most likely would view what we are going through as a blessing, not a woe. If the opinion is out there that even our troubles are worth the joys we experience, why not let that opinion be ours?

You Are the Guru

Live in a mansion? You are the guru. Live in a tent? You are the guru. Live on a mountain or below sea level? You are the guru. Nothing made available to the Dalai Lama, Gandhi, any number of Popes, Jesus, Mohammed, Moses, your teacher, the Buddha, or a man or woman secluded from our experience of the world, is any more or less than what is offered to us. It is for us to learn. It is for us to do. It is for us to teach. Anything that leads to peace. Anything that leads to love. Anything that leads to compassion. Good luck and good teaching.

The Secret

There is no secret. There is only what we need to learn (which is hard to determine) and what we need to unlearn (which is hard to admit). These things can be done on a mountain, in the streets of Calcutta, in a big bath tub in Beverly Hills, or anywhere we close our eyes, take deep breaths, and smile for no reason at all.

My wife's cousin who is in 8th grade this year asked me the question, "Why can't dinosaurs clap?"

I said I did not know.

He said, "Because they're dead".

There is no great commentary on death here. Just a joke to show that all our searching and seeking is no more than a punchline to a joke the Creator told many years ago. Be happy. Be at peace. Be for others what you needed when you found yourself there.

Love Is Not a Side Hug

I never cared much for authority. I never "just followed the rules". I enjoy others enjoying tradition more than I enjoy it myself. I walk outside barefoot in colder weather to cool down (against my mother's wishes) and i have never caught pneumonia.

I believe I have more responsibility for the good and bad things in my life than I care to admit, but do not hold others to that standard. I believe people are inherently good. I believe people are inherently bad. I believe there is only one person in the world that I can change, and in changing myself, I change the world.

And what do I know of you? No matter who you are? Most likely you struggle with some things, and you have a sense, hopefully, that you were meant for greater things. This is not quackery, a false psychic reading, pseudoscience, or pop psychology. This is me, knowing there is a greatness in you, that is expressed each time you share a smile.

Share a smile, while alone, with the
Universe, and see for yourself if the Universe does
not smile back. My experience is that it will. Not
because the Universe is dependent on your smile,
but that in your smiling, you begin to co-create joy
with the Universe that can be doled out to those
who, for some reason, have not quite yet learned to
smile.

No matter where you find yourself, you are
important. If you cannot see a better future, trust
that life will find one for you. If you cannot trust
that life will find better things for you, then at the
least, do not actively doubt life's motive. And if all
you can see is darkness, do not spread it to others. A
world of darkness is overcome with the smallest,
and I mean to say, the very smallest, of sparks.

You may feel yourself to be void of light
and at the same time be the only light another
person sees. You may be worried for things that are
since passed, and not yet see the positive future
those events have carried to your life. You may be
carrying those events to the lives of others.

What I know of Love is this. It is not content with a side hug. It wants a "seeing a grandparent for the first time in a while" hug. Love does not demand this from you, but offers it to you, every moment, every day. Love pours itself out to you by the measure in which you receive and share it. Its source is infinite, and its comfort can be found in an instant. We need not look for Love, we need only to accept Love. It is not in the seeking, but in the asking, that we find joy.

Make a small difference today and watch it grow. Notice some small, otherwise unnoticeable thing, for which you have yet to express gratitude. Make a phone call you might not make normally. Send a card or leave a note you typically would not write. Give yourself, in some small way, over to the way of Love, and test its ability to support anything you do in kindness. Smile back at Life.

Pardon my enthusiasm, but in you exists what has been for eternity. In you is the ability to change the very world that has been created for you. In you is the smile that someone has been waiting to see. And you have the potential to be the only sign a person has asked for, you may offer the only consideration that helped someone hang on for one more day, and though not acknowledged, your simple acts of kindness, will help bring healing to a world that desperately needs to be healed.

Three Simple Things

Sometimes I get caught up in worrying about my experiences being universal. Sometimes I worry that they may not be helpful at all. Regardless of those wondering(s), I sit and type from time to time, thinking there might be something from what I have learned that may help someone else in some small way. What follows are three simple things that help me smile more than I frown (though I do still frown on occasion).

Be Thankful

One thing, I do every day, is bend over. It is the one thing that makes me notice I am growing older and have new limits physically more than any other thing. Whether bending to tie my shoes or to pick something up, there comes the normal "older person" aches and pains with each effort. It used to be a real drag to pick something up off the ground.

Rather than moan and groan about my age, or the aches and pains, I say to myself, and sometimes out loud and to the Universe, "Thank you for everything I have". Or, "Thank you for peace". What used to be a way to beat myself up over my weight, age, or physical condition, has become a very real way of practicing gratitude. This has not only given me a better outlook on living, but it has replaced the dread of bending over with an enthusiasm for everything good in my life.

Give Up on Being Right

Being right is important in life. It helps us do things that matter. Most of the arguments I have been involved in, and really, the ones I have seen in the world (when I care to pay any mind to the world), center and grow around participants needing to prove they are "right". Regardless of the debate or issue, whether anyone is right has little to do with a positive solution. So much time is wasted proving

we know what we are talking about, instead of
hearing others.

There can be more than one way to do
things the right way. There can be two perspectives,
by virtue of where we are seeing things, that can be
different, and also right, at the same time. But
giving up on being right is not about believing
another person's opinion might be right, as well.
We can allow others to be wrong in our opinion
while they believe they are right. Our purpose is so
much more than making "thought-clones" out of
everyone we meet.

Contemplate a Sunflower

Sunflower, special person, fond memory, or
a great feeling you have had and would like to have
again. Any of these will work. Our minds have a
lot, and I mean A LOT of free time. Intentional, on
purpose thinking, leads to better things than letting
our minds wander into whatever vortex outside
forces thrust upon us. We can be governed by a
simple, positive thought when we find ourselves

reacting to things rather than creating joy for ourselves and others.

For me, lately, this thought is a sunflower. From time to time I look for pictures of sunflowers on my cell phone. I imagine myself in a field of sunflowers. I think of sunflowers I saw as a child riding my bicycle through our neighborhood and remember the warm breeze as I turned the corner at top speed in an effort to take the next hill with more ease. I think of those in my life, both living and passed, that love sunflowers. And as silly or useless as this sounds, it takes the place of worrying for things beyond my control.

Can It Be This Simple?

Be grateful. Be content knowing *what* we do, without having the need to convince others we know *why* we do, what we do. Be intentional about what we think about. Be hope to others, all the while knowing, that compassion is not about conformity, kindness is not about compliance, and that our happiness is our responsibility and not for others to guarantee.

Banana Seat Bandits

When I was young, though I am unsure how young, my parents bought me a Murray bicycle. It was the very best thing I had known in life until that time. While other kids on the block had a cool Huffy BMX, or some fancy 10-speed, what I rode around the neighborhood on was this Murray bicycle with coast brakes and a banana seat.

Not to say this bike did not have a lot of extras. I remember some of the best handlebar grips known to man (I was certain they were used during the lunar landing). Some plastic piece that served as a "gas tank", reflectors on the front AND on the pedals. And best of all, what made me faster than any other thing on two wheels at the time, yellow stickers of lightning bolts on both sides. I knew I was fast, because there was an after-market speedometer, as well.

One summer morning, I woke to find it gone. Panic set in, I ran in the house to the kitchen to find my mother and explained I had left it in the yard and now it was nowhere to be found. Being the mother she was, she helped me look for my ride. All the while I had my suspects running through my mind. Jealousy. Someone had to be jealous and they took my bicycle. The police were called. A report was filed. All day I worried about what I was to do and how I could replace such a wonder of land-speed record breaking.

When my father pulled in the driveway from his day's work, we rushed out to meet him. I went over the list I had made of possible suspects and my mother explained the process of how we were to claim the bike in the event it was recovered from an underground bicycle thieving ring of criminals. We talked about the possibilities of another kid taking the bike, where I had left the bike, and what I was going to do that summer without a way to get around. We talked until the sun fell over the woods in front of the house.

It was then that my father told me to go get my mom and come back down to the yard. Upon returning, he took a deep breath and said, "Come with me".

He led us to what we called the "Wood Room" in the basement. He clicked on the light and there, in the middle of stacks of kindling, upright, and on a kickstand, was the orange Murray, in all of its plastic, rubber, and metal, glory. My dad was magic. My dad had spent the afternoon knife-fighting hoodlums and hooligans to retrieve my property. My dad risked his life to make sure I had a ride that summer.

Actually, my dad had hidden the bike in the Wood Room that morning because before coming into the house the night before, I left it behind his car. Just like the times before when he asked me to put it inside the garage. He did not scold me. He reminded me once more to make sure it was put up each evening and asked if I would like to ride a little before I went to bed. Pretty sure that was so that he and mom could have some time to speak about his not letting her know where the bicycle was during the police visit.

Funny thing, after spending the day worried, searching, and speculating, my first reaction was not anger towards my father, it was relief. I did not spend the time on that after-hours ride grieving over the lost time riding that day. Somehow, the night air was sweeter, the tires sounded like music on the asphalt, and though it might be clouded by other memories, I am almost certain the speedometer reached the highest mark in the history of speedometers. Surely, I enjoyed that night ride more than I would have enjoyed riding that day not knowing what it was like to have lost the bike.

My life is like this today. The good things I am accustomed to, seem like they are deserved. The things I sometimes do without, seem like new blessings when they return. It is not for me to long for what I do not have. It is for me to be open to new blessings. Both in possessions and in joy, happiness, and peace.

The secret… and do not let this out… is to be grateful always. Do not count your blessings. There is not enough time. And while you are busy taking a tally of what you have, you might miss what is being offered anew. But, be grateful for every thought, person, and gift, that crosses your mind, every beat of the heart that God saw fit to equip you with, and every breath that fills your lungs (even the one you forgot about until just now).

You are here because the force that created ladybugs, puppy dogs, and autumn leaves, and daisies, knows you have a purpose. I suspect, that purpose is to create in others smiles that might take years to form.

Happiness

Each morning, after stumbling around to find either a cup of coffee or a Diet Mountain Dew, taking a daily dose of whatever medicine a doctor has recommended, and gathering some insight to distinguish between what was yesterday and what was a dream from the night before, I start to plan the day before me. On the weekends, this planning takes place on a deck facing a protected marsh with several trees and could be imagined to go on for miles if it was not known where the development of city storefronts begin. It is usually silent and still until just before the first rays of daylight come from the horizon behind me. Then I hear squirrels.

Just after hearing them bark, either at each other or to the new dawn, there is enough light to watch them scurry about in the trees. They jump from limb to limb, chase each other's tails, and dig in the ground below. All of this activity makes me wonder if they will have food this winter. There are so many fables about grasshoppers and ants and animals found in nature told to inspire us to prepare for the days to come. Mostly it makes me wonder if they know what they are doing. From where I sit consuming the allotted caffeine for the day, it looks a lot like they are playing and having fun.

Where do they get off, I wonder, just goofing around when there is so much work to do in life? I hope they do not expect me to feed them when there is snow on the ground. What would a squirrel have to be happy about anyway? What I have noticed, over the years, is that though squirrels appear in every way to be happy and having fun most always, they continue to flourish. And what would I know about living the life of a squirrel?

There are some people, regardless of what they "do", who are, like squirrels, happy. Some people I meet are so busy chasing after happiness with such labor-intensive desire, they do not seem happy at all. And like I ponder the life of the tree hopping, fun loving animals in the back yard, I consider what would make a person happy in the first place. Happiness is not an object. It is not a house or a car. It is not a list of friends or money in the bank. Truly, until we quit trying to view happiness as a possession, we will never experience it.

It has been said by some, "I am better than no one and no one is better than me". That seems so humble and so grounded and so connected to the Divine. It also sounds to me untrue. There is someone that is better than you. You are better than someone. Until you realize this, true happiness will allude you every morning you wake and every night you rest. Of course, the person who is better than you, is the "you" that will wake tomorrow. The person you are better than is the "you" that laid its body down for sleep. These are the only people you can please. These are the only people you can influence. These are the only people you can change.

For what it is worth, may I suggest we do everything with suspicion raised in others' minds that we are just having fun. If we are white water rafting or if we are taking out the trash, we can smile. If we are receiving a meal or offering a meal, we can do it in the name of Love. When imagining a different life or existence for ourselves, we might imagine great things and not only better things. Speak of failures as lessons, troubles as opportunities, and coincidences as divine appointments. And for the love of God, learn to accept the love of God. In many ways, happiness is in you already. The secret is to clear all of the other stuff away so that it is able to bubble up to the top.

Signal Strength

Information is everywhere. Propaganda, be it good or bad, is everywhere. It is hard not to be affected by another's thoughts or worldview. Quite frankly, it takes more courage, intention, and will power to be at least an independent thinker, or better still, a free thinker.

Our highways are littered with billboards. Our living spaces are designed around a television that pipes in, you guessed it, other people's thoughts and ideas, and our lives are centered around whether or not we "forgot our phone".

There is no value placed on quiet contemplation, because there is no way to charge for quiet contemplation. There is no value placed on "not knowing", because your worth in society requires a definition of where you stand on this or that issue. And the Divine is redefined and packaged into thirty-minute television segments and sold like snake oil. Even the air, or space, or atmosphere, is filled with signals. Marconi (or Tesla if you get right down to it) would have shuttered to think about the volume of radio waves pumped through creation.

When I was younger, I wondered if God would be pleased if I left a recording of praise music playing in my room as I went to school. As I grew older, my guess was that the Creator would actually like me to turn it off. These days I wonder what it must be like for God to have to deal with not only the thoughts of someone's mind, but those thoughts being converted to signals and spewed throughout creation.

If Christ returns, my hope is that included in the first words he says to his creation, will be, "For the love of me… please… shut up". Ironically, I am writing these words while listening to a streaming music service. Most of us, including me, do not thrive in silence. Those of us that do make time for silence more likely do it to "hear the Voice of God", which is, in and of itself, not silence.

These words are not meant to bemoan the fact that there is technology. It is not meant to over exaggerate the fact that there is little room for more information in this corner of the Universe. It is meant as a reminder to be aware of what we are taking into our minds. To be intentional about what we allow there. To take some seconds of the day to turn it down. Each day I thank the Creator for the day, wipe the slate clean, and start over in the morning. It is almost like ritual cleansing from being in a world that is beautiful by design, and that has been corrupted by greed, self-importance, and hatred.

There is a beacon flashing, a light burning, and lighthouse shining somewhere that originates from, and is, the Divine. We venerate the masters who seem to have tapped into a way to receive that signal and spread its message. We assume it was and is a weak signal. The reason we have trouble hearing its voice, is that we seek its origin in the stars or heavens, or in a text, or a teacher, as if the voice were light years away. We cannot comprehend its magnitude until, like the horror movie said about the mystery call, we realize, "It's coming from inside the house". God is in you. The very simple secret is, listen to and enjoy your guest.

If you realized the greatness you possessed, you would never listen to another critic again. Even the critic you have become of yourself. Turn down the sound on your opinion of others and yourself. You will find the Conductor of your heart playing a rhythm only you can dance to. Life may not always be easy, but at least you will be dancing.

The Switch

I never was too impressed by those that say we are able to manifest things in the world by what we think. But I have wondered lately if this might not be true. It has been said that every action begins with a thought. To me, action might be better able to manifest material things in the world and if this is the case, then all action must begin with thought and therefore thought is required before anything is made manifest in our lives.

So, what of thoughts or thinking. So many people throughout history have said so many things about "right thinking" or "guarding our minds" that quite frankly it makes me tired "thinking" about the issue of "thinking". I have certainly not mastered anything in this life, especially things of an inner or spiritual nature, but here is what I know to be true.

The cure for worry is gratitude. One can simply not be worried and grateful at the same time. Typically, we worry for the future. When we worry about our past, it is only in relation to how it will affect our future. Nothing in our pasts matter and our futures are determined by right now. And right now, the sensible thing to do is be thankful, rather than to moan and groan over what was or will be.

We are not our possessions. Nothing we own, nothing we wear (including these forms we call bodies), and nothing we do are who we are. There is in you, a spark of the Divine. There is in the Divine, you. If we (and that is all of the we(s) out there) are anything at all, we are the expression of the Creator, which please the Creator, for no reason other than we exist at all. This is a miracle. That we exist at all. All we own is fluff.

We choose what we think about. My only advice here is not to worry for what we have done wrong, but to imagine what we might do right. Do not assume you know what should be considered victory or what is defeat with regard to what you have accomplished. Spend time thinking about what good you may do today.

The small things matter. Smile. Wave. Study compassion and teach it by example. Be comfortable holding a hand other than your own. If you have power, use it for good. If you have love, do not reserve it for a few. If you have grace, give it to everyone and every situation you encounter. The world needs more of that. Do not crave an understanding of the big picture but be content in small contributions which are easily understood.

Some are daisies and some are roses. We are in a mysterious and wonderful garden. What sense would it make if a daisy and a rose fought over which was the original flower? What sense would it make for the garden if they spent their time plotting ways to kill one another? What sense would it make for them not to share the same rain, the same sun, the same soil? Share. Even with a flower whose pedals look nothing like your own.

If only there was a switch in our brains. In our lives. In our relationships. Even in our hearts. A switch that would control emotions, grief, and maybe concern. A switch we learn to turn off and on. Of course, if it did exist, it should be well guarded lest some other circumstance or person learn to flip our switch. Perhaps though, there need not be a switch. Maybe we have access to a source of power that we regulate by how much we allow it to flow through us.

Your goodness cannot be removed by those that would want you to feel guilty of crimes you did not commit. Your nature cannot be condemned as sinful by those who are not fit to judge. Your worth cannot be determined by those who fail to see your light in their darkness. What I know, and hope that you do also, is that everything is available to you.

It is as if the Kingdom of Heaven were at hand. It is as if you might only have to ask and you would receive. It is as if you were eternal and that this life, and these deaths around it, are illusions. And it is that, we may see the face of God not in the heavens, but in the stranger sleeping on the sidewalk. And we do that, because someone did that for us. Whether we are aware of it or not.

The Church at Hunt Road

Often times in my life, I have had the inward thought, that if you visit a good church, you might not know you were in church at all. And so, it was with the church on Hunt Road, when I was a child. Though faded with age, my memories of the times spent there are of a love for animals St. Francis would envy. There was a love for people by which Mother Teresa would be inspired. And the diversity of those that crossed its threshold made the Creator proud. Lessons learned there were progressive and taught with items as simple as a molasses popcorn ball.

This church had no steeple and the pastor was not paid to preach. The teachers were all volunteers. Many of its congregants were related, but one never got the sense that this relation to one another provided them with any special privilege or permissions. Holidays were celebrated with enthusiasm. Love abounded, but grace, grace was extended there as well. Education was encouraged but not required. When you stepped down the porch and into the world, you had a sense that you had somehow been changed in a way that would allow you to survive that world, until you were able to return.

Progressive? Yes. Unorthodox? Certainly. Missed? More than even I care to admit.

The church on Hunt Road was what was known to me, as Mamaw and Papaw Thompson's house. It was always a blessing to be there. Not because they spoiled me and not because they loved me without condition (though those were two great things), but because I came of age there. In a time when cell phones were fantasy. In a time where though I had so many ideas and plans in my mind, it was possible to visit there and simply, be. Sure there were days spent in hay fields, days spent hanging tobacco, and days spent tending a garden, but as it is with most tasks, the time spent with those you love is a reward regardless of how that time is consumed (this is why we learn to love those we work with, not simply the work we do).

My papaw had no need for a boat but had taken it on trade from a man that owed him money from this or that deal. I hear stories about Papaw from family and people living in Blount County. He was always making deals and from what I gather, never really for the prize, but for the love of the art of making a deal. I was older and my dad and I were going fishing. We went to pick up the boat and found my grandfather, known as Mixer to most, digging in his garden.

Thinking I knew a lot about life and that I was full of compassion, I said to Mixer, "Papaw, why do you work so hard in the garden? Why do you work so hard taking care of cattle? Why won't you take some time to go fishing with dad and me?".

He wiped his brow with a handkerchief, folded his hands and placed them on top of his hoe, "You and your dad play golf. I work in the garden. You and your dad fish. I take care of cattle."

The lesson stuck. These were things he did for enjoyment. They were not what I enjoyed, but he enjoyed them, and that was alright with him, and it was alright with me. Just after he said spoke those words, he dug a turnip out of the ground, peeled it back, cut off a piece off with his old, worn Case pocket knife, and handed it to me. From that point in my life until now, I am aware of the fact that my blessing may not be yours and your blessing may not be mine. And this is okay, even with God.

Many years later as I thought of these times spent on Hunt Road, it hit me. Papaw was not working me in a hay field because he needed the help. He did not ask me to hang tobacco because he was teaching me some life lesson. My picking vegetables from the garden was not to provide food for a meal. With everything he was, he believed we were doing something we loved, together. As years have passed, I have come to realize, though I do not bail hay these days as a hobby, we were doing things together that we loved, but it had very little to do with farming.

So, it is with life and the existence we are co-creating with the Divine. We may not have chosen a particular activity or problem to solve, but the Divine is providing a place for us to be with Itself. It may take a few years, but we will see the intent was good and not harm. That it was something enjoyable when reflected upon. And as far as the church on Hunt Road? You have not lived until you have had a molasses popcorn ball as a a communion wafer. May peace abound. May what you seek be made manifest. And may those two things be the same.

Ce Faci?

It has been my good fortune to meet a man from Moldova, named George. His English is certainly not as fluent as his Romanian, but we communicate on some levels more deeply than those around us that speak English as a first language because we intentionally communicate.

As it turns out, some of George's children went to elementary school with my son. I have heard tales of George, while visiting his kids for lunch, buying Carter an ice cream. Through field days and my visits to the school, I got to know his children and returned the favor. Carter fell, as did I, madly in love with George's family. My wife's mother, upon my first meeting George, baked him a loaf of bread and in return, George's wife sends me, from time to time, this treat or another for me to try.

I gather from some of our conversations that George has a passion for the Divine and that he might be more conservative than I am. From time to time, he sends me a link to a video of some preacher that I would not normally seek out. From time to time he will quote a verse in the Bible or admonish me that some holiday, though celebrated by mainstream Christianity, is not of God. And for every year I have known him, he has invited me to his church.

For the most part, I stay clear of public displays of worship, but last Saturday, he invited me to a baptismal service at a nearby lake. Carter wanted to go and play with his friends, so we headed out to the dam. When I arrived, there were several people gathered, all dressed much better than Carter and me. They were listening to a preacher, singers, musicians, all in a language unbeknownst to me. I stood there listening when a young woman asked, "Do you know Romanian?"

I replied "No".

She asked, "Would you like an interpreter?"

I replied "No".

Truth be told, I listen to Hindu songs and mantras that I do not know or "understand". I listen to readings of Scriptures and hymns from religions and in languages I do not understand. Truth be told, even when I go to a mainline Protestant service, the buzz words and the phrases they use baffle me. And truth be told, I am not there to hear the preacher or the musicians in the first place. Perhaps languages, like Deepak Chopra once said, are from the same root and have the same power, whether we recognize the meaning or not. Perhaps. But may I tell you about when Jesus showed up to this service?

I was standing in the sun sweating and thinking of more lofty things than I normally do. I enjoyed it. It was a great place to be at the right moment in my life. It was, though, hot and seemed to run longer than anticipated. I had not noticed that George had left my side until I felt a tap on my shoulder. George began poking my arm with a bottle of water and said, "For you. We have".

In this moment I realized. The Creator does not speak English or Romanian. He does not even, contrary to what I was taught by my Hebrew professor, speak Hebrew. There is a language spoken by The Divine that only our hearts can comprehend. Language is like using a screwdriver used to build a home. The screwdriver is not the home where we live, but it was one of many useful tools which helped us provide shelter. Whichever language we use, it is only a tool to help us live in the light of Love. It is only a tool. That bottle of water to me was the Gospel.

I have heard it said that the world is lost and dying. I also say the same thing about my car keys and the flowers just passed my porch. With effort I always seem to find my car keys and each spring those flowers are raised back to life. We are not opposed to the world, we are from the world and in the world. If our thoughts are so heavy and we think ourselves so close to heavenly things that we do not see the kingdom in any part of this life, we have missed the point. If we think that the kingdom is somewhere waiting after a time, and not, in the words of Van Halen, "Right Now", we have entirely looked over what confronts us as if it were the face of God before us. Some say, "May we have ears to hear". I might say, "May we hear without using ears at all".

Cane Pole

Fishing is not one of my hobbies. Fishing is not my way of life. Fishing is not what I have to do in order to feed my family. While I have good memories and stories to tell about fishing with friends and family, it is not something I do make time for anymore. That might be a problem I need to address in the future. There are a lot of great things about fishing.

What I do with regularity is think about and observe people and situations, sometimes to the point of absurdity. Sometimes, to the detriment of simply enjoying the moment. Some people, strolling along the river, might think of the beauty of the light reflecting off the water. Some might think about how nice it would be to swim. Some might even dip their toes in the current. And while I wish I was intelligent and "deep" enough to think of some great philosophy, I think about fishermen.

I think about fishermen in boats, who get as close to the bank of the river as they can, casting their bait to the bank, as close as they can. I think about the fishermen on the bank, wishing they had a boat, casting their bait as far away from the bank as they can. And I think of an older couple, married for years, content to simply drop their line and hook, tied to a cane pole, from a boat or the bank, into the water ten feet from where they find themselves. As far as I can tell, all with the same chance of catching a perch. All being able to go home and tell stories of how they went fishing that day.

Whether it is the fisherman on the boat or on the bank, there seems to be something that causes them to think that the fish will be away from them. I tend to live my life by this method, always running from one thing to the next, never looking for what I think I might need, within myself. I would like to be like the couple with a cane pole. Believing joy is close and can be found with little effort. It is odd really, to think we can find the fish of Joy, Compassion, Gratitude, Patience, or even the Love of God, never far from where we are along life's river, all with just a cane pole.

Vivid Imagination

Neil Young wrote a song with the words, "One of these days, I'm gonna sit down and write a long letter, to all the good friends I've known. And I'm gonna try, to thank them for all for the good times together, though so apart we've grown". It is on an album named "Harvest Moon" if you are interested. I highly recommend it.

There are times in my imaginings when I have a picnic at this or that state park or pavilion, with all the people I have met and known for a short time, those I have known most of my life, and even those I have admired and not had the good fortune to meet. You may say this is insanity and means nothing in the real world and I might agree, but it positively affects my outlook on the life I have yet to live.

At these imaginary gatherings, I might notice the leper I met in Zambia and introduce him to a business man met in Washington DC. My hope is that the business man might offer some medical relief to the leper and that the leper, in return, might show the business man how to slow down and enjoy the present moment. Perhaps the inmate at Brushy Mountain might benefit from a conversation over lemonade with a friend from my college days. And, of course my deceased mamaw would love to chat with my now wife, Michelle, about what a wonderful young man I am (I might be the only benefactor in that case).

It doesn't stop there. At times I might facilitate a discussion by a waterfall with Gandhi, Buddha, and the Christ. I speak to my friends that have passed, either by natural causes, accidents, or self-inflicted wounds and try to soothe what I perceive to be their worries or troubles. I have sung with living legends and burned out stars. I have worked in silence with my grandfather in a bailing hay, stopping only to drink the result of what ice has melted inside a plastic milk carton.

And if by now you still consider me to be sane, I will tell you of other conversations I have at my imaginary reunions. I speak with myself as a three-year old. As a preteen. As the senior in high school. The young man of 22 going through a divorce. The thirty something consumed only with a vicious cycle of work and sleep. I let them inform me of how the world looked and try to understand why they acted the way they did. Of all the people invited to the picnic, these are the only ones I have the need, and the right, to forgive, and I do.

While I know that these encounters are not real in a way that affects anyone other than me, I know also that this form of thinking is at least as harmless as entertaining myself with the evening news, a 30-minute television show filled with 10 minutes of commercials, or mindless readings of social media. Of course, the people I meet in my mind are only perceptions I have of who they really were or are. Of course, nothing comes of any of it. But it does in some small way seem to be therapeutic. And there are lessons learned from life which take years after they are taught to be learned.

I am unsure if it would be considered reflection, or meditation, or insanity, but it helps. Like the Neil Young album, I recommend it. And like the Neil Young song, whether they are living or dead, it seems a way to "thank all my good friends, for all the good times together". If it all sounds too

crazy to try, I would suggest taking at least think of
one person that meant something to you and to
whom you meant something to, and though
imaginary, have a conversation about how much
you are loved. If a movie (someone else's
imagination) can make us cry, or if a post on
Facebook can make us laugh, it is plausible that our
thoughts might help us in some small way.

Consider your mind a closet in which you
may go to pray. Consider it a temple where you
might find the Divine. Let it be a home for Love
and a sanctuary for your soul. And when life seems
overwhelming, take a deep breath and realize you
have come this far with help you know nothing
about and will make it another day with help that is
far greater than you have time to understand or the
capacity to comprehend. Often times we speak over
the Creator's voice to ask for a burning bush as a
sign.

Shelter

On the weekends, I wake up as early, if not earlier, as I typically do during the work week. This is not because I am disciplined, but more likely because I am old. In truth, it is because the weekends are fun for me and there is the hope that I might get to take a nap during the day. I spend the early morning hours either reading or watching documentaries on Netflix while thinking somehow that I am better for those activities. Today was no different, except for the fact that I indulged in a documentary on the possibility of civilizations beyond earth and a massive conspiracy to cover those civilizations up and keep them from the public.

There was a great case made for alien technology. There was a great case made for groups of people who might want to keep it secret. And ultimately the question was asked, "What would other worldly life forms think of us?".

The "us" being the whole of humanity that inhabits the earth. I suppose that is a question that people have asked, and tried to answer, for centuries. It has inspired many teachers, leaders, and individuals, to encourage the whole of earth's population to become better versions of themselves. I considered the possibilities of other worldly technology and the great implications it might have. Then, as I often do, I stepped out onto my front porch and found my thoughts immediately transition to simpler things.

My attention was drawn to two mocking birds raising immortal hell, diving and swooping towards a neighborhood cat, which was simply walking up the street. I am not a cat fan and am a little partial to birds, but I felt sorry for this particular cat. It would stop and turn towards the dive bombers who were making both their presence known and a horrible screeching noise. The cat would walk a few steps, and the birds and the cat would repeat the process. This lasted until the cat made it to the base of a Bradford Pear tree in our yard and began to climb.

The noise stopped. The birds flew away. After a minute or two, the cat came down and started walking again without the attention of the mocking birds. I began this story with great conspiracies and am ending with a cat and two birds. But the star of the story is the tree. For you see, with all of our technologies, and with all of our being busy in the world with things that may or may not be important, we can, for some short moment, be a tree for those being dogged (or birded) by life.

The secret of the masters is helping others without anyone knowing. The secret of most of our success stories, is being helped by others, whether we knew it or not. Whether we donate all our income to this cause or another, or whether we listen to a stranger tell us about their troubles for a moment in a convenient store, we can be like the tree was for the cat on my street. While I am, and I say this with honesty, not convinced there is enough desire for justice or mercy on earth to save humanity, I am convinced that if it is done, it will be by small actions, in everyday situations, and go

mostly unnoticed by all except those that are
helped.

I just checked my front yard. The tree is still there. The cat has walked away, and the mocking birds have flown to other places. The tree is still there. Whether it is providing shelter or not, it is a place of shelter. It provided shelter for the cat because that is what it is, and after the cat is gone, remains. We may be known by some for the things we do, we are able to live with ourselves because of what we are.

And just a side note to end. Most of you are great oak trees that think of yourselves as acorns. You are, by virtue of being you, providing shelter to so many already. Though you do not help others for gratitude, I will say "thank you", not on my behalf, but on the behalf of those that smile when they remember you. On behalf of those, when needing an example of kindness in order to hang on, have bumped into you. Those that are, without they, or you, knowing, have become great because of your example. You are perpetuating a conspiracy of kindness. When it is all said and done, that is the only conspiracy I enjoy.

Cathy... With a "C"

There are many reasons I am lucky to do what I do for a living. Without giving it away, I help train people with personal growth and development among other things. I also have the opportunity to meet several people in the course of any given day. At grand opening events such as the one I attended last week, I might learn (and hopefully retain) the names of over five hundred people. As you might imagine, some are more memorable than others.

My method is simple. Greet people with a smile. Take as much interest in them and their story as I hope they have in mine and ask their name before introducing myself. Volumes of books and seminars have been written and given on effective sales and customer service and I hope this short summary of "method" might save you some time and effort. One thing I might add about this simple form of customer interaction. Do not fake it. It would be better for you to be in an office doing paperwork if your only interaction with a customer is fragmented or phony.

Last week, I bent over to speak to a customer in their car and we spoke for a moment about a few things related to my offerings and a few things related to this or that topic. After Brenda shared her name, I bent lower as to see past Brenda and into the passenger seat of her vehicle. Then I saw a woman, about thirty years old, who seemed a little annoyed with my banter but also a little happy when I asked her name. The passenger responded with a firm, "I'm Cathy with a 'C'".

Brenda looked at me and smiled a slow, thin smile, as if to convey that Cathy was somehow not like the rest of the customers that I met that day. I have no inclination to know why. I have no desire to know the back story of what some might call her disability. I did not ask, and really, when if I get right down to it in my mind, I have no right to ask or even wonder what might have been her history any more than I might be compelled to know the history of any of the five hundred smiles I saw that week. What Cathy left me with, however, has changed my days since meeting her.

Cathy was eager for me to know her name. She was eager for me to know it started with a "C". She told me with an urgency and a confidence that made me want to know more, though I did not have the chance. What I do know, is that I have had the chance to meet millionaires, people with $2.56 to their name, and everyone in between. I have spoken with others about heavenly things and the basest aspects of human nature. I have heard quotes from religious leaders, dictators, revolutionaries, and children of all ages, but none said more to me about poise and confidence than Cathy. And she did it with one sentence.

I am certain that Cathy needs help with some day to day tasks. I am certain that those charged with her care might get frustrated at times. What I heard that day was someone ready to let me know her name as if I should have known it already.

As if I might have been the one uninformed if I had not yet known that Cathy was spelled with a "C". And here I am on a Sunday morning reminiscing about a chance encounter with a new friend believing that she may know more than me about customer interaction.

It is easy for us to feel we are in positions enough to pity others. It is easy for us to think we know who is disabled or who needs help. To some extent it might be a good quality for some to always fret over and be concerned for others, but to some extent it is pretentious to determine who is less fortunate. The blessings we receive are not dependent on giving or receiving. They require a giver to give to bless a receiver and a receiver to receive in order for the giver to be blessed. It is as much up to the receiver as the giver for blessings to be manifest.

Cathy and I gave each other our names. Sometimes, that is all the blessing you need. At the very least, I think of Cathy and smile. Would that not be the ultimate result of any interaction we were involved in? They say that when the student is ready, the teacher will come. Sometimes, all the teacher needs to speak is her name.

On Going Home

"Take a right at the light, go past the school and take a left. Right after that, take an immediate right and I am the seventh house on the left. It is the only house with landscaping lights."

Those words amazed me. I can still hear them now. This woman, a girl in some ways, was describing how I could find her before our first date. Little did I know, or really, likely did I know, that this house would become my home. I mowed the yard several times before I lived there. I returned from many nights out to drop off my then girlfriend. I met the children that would become my kids. I met the dogs that would become my pets. I shared popcorn and movies, home cooked meals, and enjoyable conversation with the love of my life in this house. A house that was bought after a divorce, in a bit of a rush, by a person never knowing, as divorcees often are not knowing, if she would ever find love again.

When I needed to know her ring size, I borrowed a tape measure and pretended to measure the back door for the addition of a storm door. Secretly, I slipped into the bedroom and measured one of her rings to compare to a engagement ring. She was so disappointed that she did not get a storm door that later I had to purchase one. This home is where she smiles. This home is where we fight, and cuss, and hug, and do life together. This home is where Taylor and Tiffany grew up and out, and where Carter found a love he had not had before. It is a house that contractors built, but a house that shelters love.

We signed papers to sell the home this week. A day later it was sold to one of two buyers that made an offer. Some people bake cookies before someone looks at their home for sale. We packed it with thirteen years of love. I will not miss the home. I have left it before (another long story). In truth, it is, and never was, my home. My home is in the heart of those that will travel with me through life and into another house. My home is in the Creator from whom no matter where I go, I cannot escape. Still, it is where I became who I am for some years of my life.

I will place my head in a pillow tonight thinking about what it means to go home. Thinking about where my home might really be. I will go to sleep tonight, as I often do, with thoughts of those without a home. I will dream with wonder about the Universe and the small part I play in its speaking to its creation. And when I wake, I will either be excited that I made it through another night of rest, or I will be excited that I am with my Jesus in a way I have not known before.

As for going home, I am unsure if I have ever had a home. I am unsure if I have ever belonged anywhere. And in that uncertainty, I find that I am home wherever I am. It all looks the same when your mind is fixed on other things. And while my aspirations and responsibilities create more for me, I am content with Spotify, a book or two (audio and otherwise), a pair of wireless headphones, and access to the sermons of my favorite clergyman Don Morris. What blesses my soul is knowing that when I sleep and when I wake, the love of my life, just a few turns and seven houses away, thirteen years ago, will be within reach.

They say that home is where the heart is. They say so many things. I have left parts of my heart in so many places, countries, and with so many others, that I have lost track of where my home might be. What I do know, is this house, while it may not be my home, means something to me. Just as the next house I live in will mean something to me. We trick ourselves in thinking that we are physical beings with a soul. It must be that we are souls with physical forms. And this is the conundrum with housing. I am moving into a new house, but it is only another tunic for my home. I never had a dream home. I have, however, been lucky enough to have a home to dream in.

My Mamaw Had a Baby

She had been my grandmother all of my life.
For as long as I could remember. Those days at the
end of her life were different than the days of my
childhood. I did not run to her and hug her. I did not
climb into her lap and learn to draw simple
renderings of birds. I did not ask for angel food
cake and she did not offer me ice cream. My mother
did not take me to see her, but I made time to drive
myself to a nursing home in the north end of town.

I would find her speaking to her child.
Sometimes in her bed that was one of four in a
room and sometimes slouched in a wheelchair
making the circuit around the facility. We might go
to the cafeteria or we might wheel out into the
courtyard, but we always spoke about things as if
she had an inclination of what was happening.
There were no indications that she did. One week
she lost her glasses. The next she lost her teeth. One
week, the most disturbing of all the weeks, she lost
her baby.

My Mamaw Bonnie, loved everyone she met. Everyone except her baby loved her in return. It was the kind of love that taught you how to love. The kind of love that once given, took on a life of its own. She made people better versions of themselves. She raised seven children, one of which was my mother that followed her footsteps not only in the way she lived, but into the same halls of that same nursing home. She touched the life of everyone… except that baby.

In truth, it was a baby doll. I am fairly certain we found it eventually in the care of another patient and returned it my grandmother. For all the love she had in her life before, and with all the confusion from dementia setting in, the last years of my mamaw's life was spent loving that baby. Love. It seems simple and it may be, but every visit there, included that baby. This baby she would speak to without conversation in return. This baby that needed nothing but that garnished all of that love from a saintly woman.

I think of her and my mother at times in heaven. Visiting. Sharing. Speaking of things both of earth and God. My thought is that they are now completely in God, where they would feel most at home, because they were, and are, two of the godliest people I have known in my life. And just as I visited her in her sleeping or waking hours without her knowing, and her not recognizing I was there, I am certain they visit me in mine. Just as I checked on her well-being, I am certain those two women still check on me, in this nursing home we call life.

My mamaw had a baby. In the end, that is to what her worldly possessions amounted. In the end, she owned nothing. Her life was not, and will not, be measured by what she had, but by what she meant to, and did for, others. This is success. I miss my grandmother and all those close to me that have passed, and quite frankly, death sucks. It is not really an end for those who die, but it is an end in the way the living can relate to them. That is the hard part.

May we realize that most of our pursuits are as silly as that baby, no matter what we might think of them. May we understand that others care for their pursuits as much as my mamaw cared for that baby. May we love and be loved before we lose the chance.

Memories in the Present Moment

I would love to consider myself a student of religion. I have a degree and everything. I would love to consider myself a student of all religions. It does not compromise my belief. It does not hinder my ability to love and be loved by Christ (cats out of the bag… I am a Christian in most senses of the word). If there is a truth found in Buddhism, it is truth. If there is truth found in Kabbalah, it is truth. If there is a truth found in Hinduism, it is, by all means, truth. To prove I have a degree, I will quote Meister Eckhart.

"If God were anything other than truth, I would flee from God and cling to truth"

That is probably a paraphrase, as my attempt to prove I am educated is halfhearted at best. So where does this leave me? How can I claim a truth found in Southern Baptist doctrine and also in an inexplicable explanation of the Tao? To what do I cling in times of trouble and to whom do I turn with questions of spirituality? And as all Christian denominations would want to ask, how do I get my checks to God? What, in the world, am I left with, when I have no group to affirm my decisions or leave me feeling justified?

May I say, while all of the feel-good language I use in my writings and on my social media posts can be tied to experience, either that of my own or others', most of what I write is recycled. The reason I bring up my being a student, or at least an observer, of religions, is that most of what I write or feel about God can be found both in sacred texts and also in several manifests of late sixties and early seventies cults. Just as most of what is preached in mainstream religions today and what was preached in those aforementioned cults, sound eerily the same.

As a society, I have noticed, we are no longer afraid of "cults". We think John Travolta and Tom Cruise are just "the berries" because they are involved in Scientology. We assume since the Mormon Church has made it this far, that watching Sister Wives on A&E is just another form of entertainment. There are no Dateline specials on deprogramming and rarely any expose on any group until there is a murder suicide or mass killing. I do not advocate witch hunting, but at least back in the day, there was a debate about such things.

Brainwashing used to be a real concern. Something that was combated. Something to be guarded against. Heaven help us all. Though it was misguided at times (in the early nineties I was told I could not be a Christian and a free mason simultaneously) at least there was a sense that there might be "right thought" and "controlled thought". Guess what? We are all brainwashed. Like it or not, admit it or not, we allow ourselves to absorb any catchy jingle or song, advertising campaign, or media news of the minute. If you don't believe me, try putting your cell phone in a drawer for three days without shaking.

I am not talking about thought that is correct or incorrect, left or right, conservative or liberal, I am talking about free thinking. The process of using our own studies and our own experiences to form an opinion. And here is a magnificent notion, what if we all reserved the right to "not have an opinion" on any given topic the busy world throws in our face. What if we simply did not know if Target should let a man use a restroom designated for women. What if we acknowledged that Hirambe may have died justly or unjustly, but that we simply do not have an opinion on his death.

We are cast into a world each day that demands so much of us while guided by a God that demands so little. When faced with a decision we cannot figure out, you know God may not care if we get a large or small Starbucks in the morning, what if we were able to ask ourselves these questions. Is it kind? Is it responsible? Is it going to harm anyone other than myself? Will I worry over it tonight before bed? And lastly ask this. Will it create in me a joy that I might be able to share with others?

If these questions can be answered with satisfactory responses, realize that you have more than one right choice to every situation. Know that you are a gift to God and others. Know that your smile is important to your well-being, God and others. Know that if you perceive beauty, at that moment, you become a part of that beauty. At that moment and before, even after, you are a part of beautiful creation.

The point of what Christians call "The Last Supper" or "Eucharist", was not the sipping of the cup or the digestion of the bread. It was, if you recall, to be done in, remembrance. In an act of defiance against all, and pardon my nonreligious vernacular, the "ca-ca" that the world wants to cram into our brains, remember him. Worry not for what Jesus would do. Breath deep. Love big. And without a cup or loaf, help others remember him.

Worlds Away

In my early years on this earth, I had the good fortune to travel to different cities in the United States, and the world, with groups of people who were determined that what they had to offer was what those cities needed. Primarily, the focus was religion. Specifically, a Southern Baptist portrait of Jesus. Even early on in life, there was something in me that would not allow me to be "spoon fed" any information about God. It was never that I opposed the notion of the Divine, but always that the notion was preached with an "us and them" mentality. Always with the "us" being superior.

There were several cities and several projects, but the Zambian trip was to be my last official mission trip with any organization. The leaders of these trips were often frustrated with my tendency to wander off with locals as they would show me their homes or work places. There was always a good chance I would be in a nearby field playing games with children or down the road with those working close to a project site, rather than being one of the forty students assigned the task of painting a small room. In Zambia I realized, I had flown thousands of miles away with the intent of teaching Zambians what they already knew. A gospel of a Christ that had been there before me for centuries.

My perspective on my home town changed. Though I had seen the view from the top of the largest water fall in the world, there were sites as beautiful found on my return home. The faces I saw in other towns and countries were on the streets of the city where I was raised. After most of these trips, I found the only thing that had changed for the better or worse, was me. There is room in this world and in the Creator for those who help at home and for those who help abroad, but for me, it was obvious that most of my trips were simply working vacations and that it was up to me to *learn from* them more than I *taught while on* them.

I am not the Great White Hope. And for so many reasons, neither is Jesus. There will need to be many things other than religion offered to other cities and countries if the world will grow together. But that involves relinquishing of power and control, and to be quite honest, I do not see governments or religions doing any of that well in the near future. "Give a man a fish and he will eat for a day. Teach a man to fish and he will eat for a lifetime". It saddens me, but I believe the world has taught men to fish so that the world might have an over-abundance of fish. As for Jesus not being the Great White Hope, he is not white, but he is the hope. He may be the answer, but we need to start seriously considering the questions.

All is not lost. My times on those trips were not wasted. No time ever is. Each day, each moment, each new truth about the Divine, even each new truth we discover about ourselves, should be like a five-pound diamond we found in our backyard. We should want to share it. Have it appraised. Protect it from theft. And though it too would be passing, enjoy the feeling we get when we think of it. If we get excited enough about our chicken dinner to post it on social media for all of our friends to see, how much more should we smile at a stranger because our creator nudged us this morning and said, "Wanna go again."?

It is this. We are worlds away from one another, not by virtue of distance or oceans, but by the way we treat and view each other. My hope has become that I will see the me in you, and you might see, the you in me. God is not going to be angry if his children get along for a time without mentioning the name of God. My time with my sister is not spent talking only of my father and how much my father has meant to us, or how much my father has done for us, or quoting the great things my father has said, or comparing the things our father has given her instead verses me. God is our father. He loves us. We love each other with that same love, regardless of the reasons why.

And a final note, the Creator never asked you to pass a test before he called you a child of God. Do not ask that of others. Peace be to you.

The Learning Well

You would not know it by looking at it now. Thirty or more years of brush and trees surround its perimeter. If you were not looking for it you might never know it was there or know the joy of how it was made. You might, in fact, think it was just another spot, in another yard, in another town, in any country in the world. But it is a Learning Well, where lessons learned as a young man, continue to teach the older man I have become.

When I was into fishing, I thought it might be ideal to have a pond nearby. The wet weather streams in my neighborhood caused me to think about what it would be like to have a pond in my backyard. What better way to have a pond, than to have a well to feed the pond? What better way to have a well than to dig a hole? Upon hearing my ideas on the matter, my father handed me a shovel and, I assume, laughed under his breath as I walked away.

I dug. I dug a lot. As luck would have it, my father was the type of father that wanted to spend time with me regardless of what activity I chose. My digging turned into our digging. My project became his, as well. We got more tools. We developed a pulley system out of an old swing set. After he came home from work and on weekends, we dug. In the heat of summer and at peak hours of sunshine, we dug. Our next-door neighbors would swim in their pool and ask us to join them and we declined, as we were working on bigger things.

We had to make two levels in our well, as our ladders became too short to climb in and out. We eventually had to borrow a bell pump and get rain water out before we started each day because the well became so deep. We spent a summer, an entire summer, digging what would, over time, be known as, "the well", though there was never any water struck. We never lost interest, but as we looked up at the sky through 18 feet of what was essentially a hole, it seemed like the walls might cave in. One day we just quit.

So, was it a hole or a Learning Well? It was a Learning Well and more. My father taught and I

learned. And if I was guessing, I may have done a
little teaching myself. We grew up together there.
He was taking in my younger outlook on living and
me seeking advice about the then unknown. We
laughed. We talked. We rested. We worked. If those
were the only things we learned, that would have
been enough, buOn t as I look back on those days,
when nothing mattered except the process and not
the goal, where we knew when we woke up what
we were going to do, regardless of if it mattered, it
makes me pause.

Some Buddhist monks spend hours making
beautiful artwork out of sand and then sweep it
away. They're thinking is that everything, even the
beautiful thing they created, is impermanent and
this is a way to detach themselves from worldly
things. My father, while digging the Learning Well,
carved himself into my soul. And while the well is
now just a part of some yard, somewhere, there is
nothing that can sweep him away from the core of
who I am. That is not parenting, that is God-ing. It

could have been anything, but it was a well. Or rather, the digging of a well, that shaped who I am.

Do not look for water. Do not look for love. In fact, do not look for anything, but enjoy the digging. The riding around in a car. The bed times and the bath times and the times in between. When you look at a flower, enjoy the beauty and the smell. Do not worry about how it got there or what will happen after you are gone. And in times of trouble, breathe in what breath you have and be at peace, for troubles will come and they will pass, just as the well is over grown and the Buddhist art is swept away. But the you, that is you, that is you, will be both a home to others and a permanent resident in others' hearts. Love boldly. Extend grace. Live now. This is my wish for you.

Pink Salad and a Paper Plate

A few summer days of my childhood were spent just down the road and to the right of my home. It was easy enough to walk to if you cut across a field owned by a church, but mostly my mother would pack us up in a car and we would drive to her friend's house, who as it happened, had children around the ages of my sister and me. There was a pool. There was a piano. There was the latest gaming system where I attempted to master "Donkey Kong". There was also a Siamese cat that was always suspicious of me, and me always of it.

I assume that most people have memories fixed in their minds of certain events in their lives in a way that hold particular moments in time captive. That in some way when they return to those moments in their thoughts, they travel through space and time and are transported there, and also bring that place and those remembered to the present. I assume, perhaps incorrectly, that if a moment lives in your memory, it lives also in the current goings on in life. One such memory for me is of pink salad and a paper plate.

We had a pool side picnic. My mother brought, as she often did to such events, a concoction of Jello, marshmallows, pineapples, and maybe even cherries (I have not had it in such a long time). My sister and I could not get enough of the stuff. After meals when it was served, it was not uncommon for her, and me, to have a plate of only pink salad for dessert. The four kids were at a picnic table. The older boys on one side and the younger girls on the other. My sister had her paper plate of pink salad and Brian decided to swim. Thinking that was a good idea, I got up from the table also.

What followed was my first lesson in physics. My first hint that sometimes laughter may need to be suppressed. And also, my first realization that mothers do not always care about intent when angry about results. As I got up, the picnic table acted like a see-saw. A very powerful, well oiled, see-saw. The result was my sister and our friend were flat on their backs, and I can still see pink salad covering my sister's chest. Of course, she cried, and of course I laughed, and of course, Brian and I were to blame. What is funny to me as a parent now, is hearing my mother defend Brian vehemently and Brian's mother, Janice, take up my defense.

Those times were good times, and because of those good times, these days are good times. This whole story started out as an ode to Janice Bruce and how she has been a friend to my family. A friend to me. When I realized there was no way I could recount what she has meant to me over the years or what little things she said which affect me still today, I thought it best to write about pink salad and a paper plate. I would love to end the story with a great quote about not knowing how you are going to affect people and the mysteries of the Universe and the Creator, but I must say this.

Janice told the first "Dad Joke" I ever heard. One of her kids had an issue on a particular day with their shorts riding to high. They, as any kid would, reached around, grabbed the back of their shorts and proceeded to pull them out of what we called as children, their crack. Janice asked them the question, "Are you going to the movies?"

I was excited. Back then, movies were a great treat. They answered "No." (I have to believe this was not the first time they had heard the joke).

She then asked, "Then why are you picking out your seat?"

As for the kids in the story? I believe we have all turned out well. I believe we all have love in our lives that transcends what we could create on our own. It is not that our mothers' love is what sustains us, but it is that they taught us seek a sustainable love. A love untouched by anything in this life but which provides all that is worth gratitude. And one of the things I am most grateful for, is Janice Bruce. Just another name to some, a gift from God to me.

We Are Not Echoes

Sunday mornings for me are usually spent reflecting on some thought or theory I might have had bouncing around in my head the week prior. This week my question to myself was, "How am I to be a reflection of God's grace to those I meet in the world?".

My mind drew me to the questions of how others are in need. It drew me to what I have that others might be in need of. I drew me, eventually, to those times in my life I was in need. When God met me where I was, with what I needed at the time. I was embarrassed when I realized there were very few times that I had prayed for some physical relief and was then relieved.

When I am stumped or perplexed (and it happens often), I step out onto my front porch and think. In the budding daylight, as I made my way to the porch, I noticed on the driveway two birds. Chirping. Gathering material for some nest somewhere. I kept thinking and worrying that I had not asked God for things and may have missed what was given to me. One of the birds hopped over to the porch close to where I stood worrying that the things I have were not given because I constantly petitioned and gave thanks.

Then I remembered. "Look at the birds of the air: they neither sow nor reap nor gather into barns, and yet your heavenly Father feeds them. Are you not of more value than they?" Jesus said that (though most likely not in Old English). Then back to my original question of how to be a reflection of God's grace… I decided that I should not. I decided that God had not called me to be His or Her reflection. That all those with needs that are not my own are not my problem.

But they are my opportunity. I am not a reflection of the Divine. I am a part of the Divine. And the Divine is a part of me. We are parts of the same vine which might provide food and shelter. We are a part of the same voice that might encourage. The same ear that might listen to woes. We are a part of the same heart that might share the joys of others for others' sake. We are not an echo of the voice of some religious leader that lived so many years ago. We are participants in the healing of a broken world.

So I quoted Jesus. Now I will quote Kris Kristofferson.

"Broken babies. Broken homes. Broken hearted people dying every day. How'd this happen? What went wrong? "Don't blame God."

I swear to God I heard Him say. "Not in My Name. Not on My Ground. I want nothing but the ending of the war. No more killing. Or it's over. And the Mystery won't matter anymore."

We have made a mess of things, yet there continues to be grace.

We are not echoes of God's grace. We are simultaneously the reason grace is needed and the way grace is conveyed. Both the problem and the solution. The thing about Grace is that it concentrates on the possibilities and not the reasons it was needed. The good thing about God is that whether you know it or not, whether you are grateful or not, whether you ask or not, His grace has found you. Give it away.

Aww, Hell

Through my childhood years, my high school years, and even in college, my time was spent on how I could "reach the lost". How I could help those I met "come to Christ". I spent countless nights at Long Branch Saloon shooting pool, playing foosball, and drinking Diet Coke. All while wearing a t-shirt with some Bible verse and cutesy cartoon. All the while thinking that if there were people in the bar, they needed to hear about God, from me.

In hindsight, I realize that I learned more from the friends I met there than I most likely I taught them. I have asked some questions in the years that followed. So, what became of them? And what becomes of them? Did I fail in some great mission? Am I failing even still by not trying to convert every soul I see? And for some reason, among all of these questions, I am reminded of one asked of me years ago. Will I see Gandhi in heaven?

The question has also been asked of me, is there a hell? Much like there was or was not a dinosaur, the grace and sacrifice of Christ has made the point moot. And if there is a hell, and Christ preached there three days after his earthly death, then who am I to say he might not go back with the same intention? If you or a loved one, only became a follower of God to avoid hell, then you or a loved one, are doing it wrong.

By the same token, if you as a Christian, shape your world view or plan your day around the idea that hell exists (and is hot, and bad, and stinky), you may miss the love of God, the salvific work of Christ, and the grace given to all who live, that we are called to extend. Isn't that the problem with God letting Gandhi into heaven? That he did not earn it by saying some prayer or asking Jesus "into his heart"?

If God offered compassion and divine love to all who took a breath here on earth and extended that same love and compassion to the after-life, wouldn't that mean we are to do the same? I suppose that somehow that would mean we were not special in any way by the fact that we claim to follow Christ. Or, that means, that following Christ might mean more than going to church, reading a sacred text, or saying a prayer of repentance.

There is enough hell on this earth without me concerning myself with a hell in the future. If that is hard to believe, then take a look around. And in the example of Christ descending into hell, we might want to go across town, or to a famine ravaged area in the world (which might very well be the same place) and offer relief. Perhaps spend less of our money on little plastic bottles of water and more money on wells for people that travel three hours each way to get five gallons of clean water each day. Maybe finding the blessings our lives and trying to share them.

For the record, these words are written for me. These admonishments are mostly for me. And for the record, I feel like my mother and Gandhi are together right now telling jokes about how seriously I take myself sometimes.

Home

There have been times in my life, that I have chosen to walk rather than ride. To labor instead of rest. To help rather than turn away. There have also been times in my life, when I chose not to do the things that would lead to the comfort of others rather than myself. Lately, I feel less optimistic about a bright future and more like I need rest after a long journey. More like the torch should be passed rather than be tended to. In my youth, a drop meant many ripples that could change the world. As I age, it only means something is leaking.

With that said, might I share my quest for the home of the Divine? In my travels, I have wondered about where one would find the Creator. This all powerful and infinite being who, in His or Her wisdom, set the universe in order, all while caring enough to see that no bird goes unfed and no flower goes unclothed. I have asked that question of myself and others as I have grown.

I was always instructed to take my hat off in the house of the Lord. I have been to many temples, cathedrals, mosques, churches, chapels, sanctuaries, and synagogues. All looking for God. All with being promised that God dwells there. Always leaving with the feeling that while God might visit, these were certainly only houses at best, that humanity thought the Creator might like.

Would I find God living in Heaven if I was able to visit there? Perhaps, but I do not think that is where the Divine feels at home. Some say that nature is the place they find God. He may indeed visit there on the weekends, but I always feel so badly for those stuck in big cities. Could the home of God be the birthplace of Jesus, Mecca, or underneath a Bodhi tree? Perhaps the Dalai Lama keeps the maker of all things in his laptop.

Where is the home of God? My opinion is that the very ruler of all things lives inside each and every one of us. The question then arises, why are some so kind and some lack compassion? Why would some kill while others would help the living? Why, if God lives in us all, would there be prejudice, greed, violence, and those without homes and food? I do not believe it is a matter of whether or not God lives in you, I believe God does.

What do I ask of God? What would I do if the Creator dwelt in me? Imagine the things we could do. Imagine the people we could help. Imagine the joy it would bring. Most of us, however, myself included at times, ask nothing of the power that is in us.

At most, we ask him to hold our list of wants like we would ask a refrigerator to hold our child's third grade art project. We ask that the One that loves us most and in the best way, listen to us go on and on about the troubles of the day and how badly we want things to change. We ask that the One who created time hold just one second while we finish looking at Facebook or for a commercial. Maybe we ask him to be a coat rack for the emotional baggage we just cannot let go of.

We hold the perfect inside our imperfection. We hold all power in the selves that grow fatigued. We have and endless supply of Love we are so reluctant to share. So when I see my spouse, or a child, or a stranger living on the streets, or someone I do not enjoy, or a politician I do not agree with, or someone unlike me in every way, I have found the home of God. God is also in me. My hope is that I make it a good home. My hope is that maybe, just maybe, someone might see that this is where He or

She lives. This might be a sermon, but it is Sunday after all. May you see the grace you have been afforded, the blessing you are to others, and the light at the end of the tunnel.

The "In Between"

Sometimes I wonder to myself how things work in this world. Not the everyday things like internal combustion engines, smart phones, or city water systems, but the things that are not so easily seen or studied. Is it that God in His heaven reaches down or is it that we in our very mortal shells reach up? Does a tree reach towards the sun in its quest to expand, or does the sun draw it somehow? Do we receive blessings because of our petitions, belief, or work ethic, or are we blessed by the random acts of kindness performed by the Divine?

It has been my inclination in the past to think of such matters with both sides in mind. While wondering why I have not the things of a richer man, I keep in mind the things I have in abundance that another may not have. When I am grateful for one thing or another, I try to remember those that might lack. And if I were honest with myself, while I express gratitude for anything, I imagine myself living without it so as not to become attached or hurt if it goes away. I also wonder at times, how in the world I get anything done with all of this going on my mind.

May I say, that as a Christian, I understand that the notion of the Christian story seems unbelievable. There are times when even I, a man who has tried to base his life on the teachings of Christ, do not believe the "stories". I am suspicious of religious institutions to a fault, I doubt most claims of supernatural intervention, I do not give to building funds or offering plates for the sole fact that I think organized religion has strayed very far from what God ever intended it to be. What I do believe is that God can create miracles from our everyday simple acts. That He only requires the faith of a tiny mustard seed not because He believes that we need faith, but that is all He needs.

So, what does my mind settle down to with regard to how my Jesus and I interact with the world? Where does this leave me when I try to find enough peace to sleep? My comfort comes from the Creator and me finding one another in the "in between". I do no tire myself with exhaustive meditations, prayer exercises, or in-depth studies of one particular sacred text or another. I simply open my eyes when I wake, open my door when I leave, open my mind when speaking, and open my heart when I see a need. This frightens so many people, but I have found it is the way to find that the God you seek was caring for you all along.

Do not judge. But if you must judge, do it with empathy and compassion. Even when judging yourself.

Give others the best of you. Even when ordering a hamburger. Even if serving a hamburger. God loves you for so many reasons. Let others see why.

Be aware that things are rarely what you perceive them to be when making big decisions.

Be kind. One small act of kindness is all the effort the Divine will require of you and is all the Divine needs to multiply what you begin.

Be amazed. By the good and the bad. Living is exciting, happy, stuff. Get your hands dirty, try new things, and smile until your face hurts. It looks good on you.

Another Town

I never quite bought into the concept that those that have passed "live on" in our hearts. It never made sense that authors of print or music would be forever present in this world because of the stories or music they created before they died. And it never seemed much solace to me when well-meaning people would say things like, "You have a lot of great memories". Most of my concerns deal with the fact that I know by experience, that while everyone might recommend that we learn from the past, the "now" is all there is.

As to those living on in our hearts, there tends to be less room and time in our hearts these days. In the case of my mother, it was easy to carve out time in my week to drive with her to go shopping and have lunch or stop by and talk. There was real communion. There was a real hug. There was real conversation. I could get her a Sonic Slush and she could ask about the family and work. Yes, as for those living on in our hearts, if it is the truth, it is not the same, and quite frankly, does me little good.

I do not study the lives of musicians much and I certainly do not plan my life around the songs or commentary of celebrities. For some reason, however, the sudden death of Tom Petty floored me a little this year. I had the general impression that he was a good guy and yes, even the good guys die, but perhaps it was that his albums and songs have accompanied my adult life in some form or another. Michelle and I have very different tastes in music, but we could always agree on Tom Petty. Do I think he is still in the world because of his recorded works? I do not.

I have always been suspicious of memories. The first thing a memory might do is take me back to a time in the past in order to escape the possibility and demands of the future. That always made me nervous. The second thing about a memory that causes me to pause is that because they are memories, they most likely are corrupted by my ability to remember them. I have told the same story before to myself and others for thirty years only to find out the characters present in my story thirty years ago claim they were in other cities at the time.

My heart is too full to individually house those that have passed, and I would rather share an embrace with my mother than have her dwell there. While I still listen to Tom Petty's music with the same wonder, awe, and appreciation, he does not have the ability to make more. And memories seem only to be a trick for my mind to drift into another space. With all that said, there for me is hope.

My Teacher once told me the Kingdom of God is now. He also told me to love others. He told me to ask and I would receive. If I believe anything, it is this. Those that have left us, pass into what I call "another town in the Kingdom". They may not be in this city, but they are still in God and in His kingdom. And because all in the kingdom is in God, and God in it, my mother, Tom Petty, my grandparents, and even Gandhi (for those who are concerned about the list of who I might think enters the gates of heaven), are with us all when we are with the Creator. So, my heart is open for God, my ears are open for music, and my memories can inform and teach me how to exist in the present.

These things are of some comfort to me. May they be of some comfort to you.

Cool, But Not in a Cool Way

Some say that times were simpler back in the day. Some say that technology has made everything easier since then. As far as it matters, I say things are definitely different, but with regard to simpler or easier, there is still struggle for every human and still suffering in the world. The hope, it seems, is that each case of suffering and every struggle might still have the same root solution even if it does not have the same face on the problem.

Let's talk about snowflakes. It seems like a catch phrase to label those growing up today with this term. It says more, however, about the person using the phrase than it does about the generation they are describing. When I see twenty somethings parading in the streets protesting this or that, I do question their motives, but at the same time, I think about older people who boycott a business because someone did not say, "Merry Christmas" and instead said, "Happy Holidays". We are all snowflakes in some area of our lives.

War. As I was walking through an Atlanta airport recently, I heard a recorded message from the mayor of the city welcoming all the members of the armed forces who served and who are serving. War makes you tough. War makes you revered by most in the country today. I imagine that it is a cultural response to how poorly the nation treated their own when they came back from the Vietnam

War. The pendulum has swung the other way. One day I hope there is a recorded loop from some mayor who welcomes peace activists to their fine city, but I will settle for the day when it is silent. We all are both warriors and people who want peace at times.

So, there you have it. Warriors and Snowflakes. Two extremes. I was neither when I grew up. My only problem was to what extent if any, I was considered "cool". For the record, I was never even close to being cool. To my credit, I was aware of that fact. What I did was notice, but not emulate, were the other kids that were cool. They fascinated me. Then I went home and grew up, did my homework, and believe it or not, talked to my family. In between all of that, I played a little basketball. It was cool, though I was not "cool".

Now I am grown and have a wife and kids. Some of my family have passed and some I still get to enjoy. I hang around and speak to teens and twenty somethings. I speak with those that have been to war or have been asked to prepare for war.

We do not speak about a lot of issues or past horrors. What we do speak about is how they are doing. How their kids are doing. What was school or work like that day. If it comes up, we might ask ourselves how God feels and what He wants for us, but for the most part, we are content to be with each other without inviting our egos. We are alright.

I have often wondered if God ever learned English or if He decided it was not worth the effort. I am certain he can convey what he wants to be known without a particular language. But if there was something to be said, it might be, "You have and will make mistakes. You have and will be loved. You have been and will be alright. Help others to understand that".

Life is serious. Just not serious enough to weigh yourself down with living the notion of what you might think is "cool".

Summer of '78

Everyone has memories of this or that event in time in their lives. Some milestone or another.

Most of my memory comes to me as if I was squinting to peek through a small hole in a privacy fence. I was never a fan of pictures growing up, and even now I do not trust them much. My thought was that if something was worth remembering, I would do so at some point in time without the aid of a photograph.

Of course, I grew up in a time when a Kodak 110 was about the only technology a child could be trusted with. Click. Turn the dial. Twenty-two more pictures left. You had to think a little about what you were trying to capture on film. For better or worse, it was different than the gigabytes of images you can capture in an instant with cameras in the pockets of almost every adult and a large majority of children today. Perhaps we have forgotten how to live because of our compulsive desire to "capture life" on our phones.

With that said, I admit, my memories are in large part, not image based. There is the smell of the fresh cut grass around Fountain City Ball Park. There is the feeling I got when after catching a fly ball, the coach offered some sort of praise. It was the pride that came with the accomplishment of finding a four-leaf clover before my dad in between a double header. And as strange as it sounds, it is the taste of the mustard on a chili dog from Smoky Mountain Market which we bought "five for a dollar". The hug of my mother, the hand of my father resting on my shoulder, the dark of a night filled with "Foxes and Hounds" with my sister and friends.

I go back there from time to time in my mind. I am glad I did not know then what I know now. By the same token, I am glad I do not know now what I will in ten years. Pictures are for the ones that need a push to remember the good or bad times. That is fine. What takes me back is a taste, a smell, a voice, a person going through what I may have gone through back in the day. And as tempting as it is to spend the rest of my days in the past, where I tend to remember only the good, it is also good to take a deep breath and see the beauty of today. And what that beauty is for me may not be what it is for you. That is fine, too.

What I would like more than anything is to be a part of making someone's memory of today as good as the memories I have of the past. If my smile could do, for someone, what the smiles I have captured in my mind from the past have done for me. If my conversations could leave someone happier than when we began speaking. If the love I have received could be shared with others in a way that they may not have realized they received it until years later. My hope is that what I do today might make someone's 2017 as meaningful as my summer of '78. So, may I keep the good of what I have been through tucked away in my soul to enjoy and create in others good for them to tuck away in their souls as well.

On Gratitude

If my life were a road map, I would not be where I am by taking the fastest route. The lines on the map which designate roads would be filled with

zigs and zags and curves and very few straight lines.
At first glance, the map would seem to have
impossible mountains to climb, rough seas to
navigate, and valleys where the shadows of death
pressed heavy on the earth. That is, if my life were a
road map. As it is now, I am simply taking a
journey that has led me, mostly, to be content, to
have more than I deserve, and to be at peace with
the path that I have taken.

There was a time after my first divorce that I
lived with my parents and worked the night shift on
a truck dock. I came home from work, woke up the
next day, went to work, and repeated until the
weekend, when I went golfing with my dad. Four
years of the same routine. Four years of secretly
wanting more. Four years of relative obscurity with
regard to anything social. At night, before I fell
asleep listening to this or that Bob Dylan CD, I
would pray, as I still do, starting with the almost
rote statement, "Thank you for everything you have
given me."

After that statement in prayer, I would wonder with God if there was more. I would wonder what I could do for a living different than what I was doing then. I would wonder if there was a woman in the world that could love me as a wife would love her husband. I would wonder if it would be possible to own a home. With God, I would wonder, not so much worry or fret, but imagine the possibilities for my life. My imaginings never reached the "planning" stage until much later, as I never quite saw how any of the things that I wondered about would become a reality.

Every night, before falling asleep, "Thank you for everything you have given me."

Ten years later, I still start my prayers with that same, almost rote, thanks giving. And to be honest, I spend a lot less time imagining the things that might be different for me. For the sake of honesty, my imaginings are more bewilderment as to how it is possible that I, coming from where I was, made it to where I am. My wife and I have had ups and downs, but our love has always given us reason to pause, find the love we have for each other, and continue on. I have had the honor of helping to raise three children, two of whom are now adults. I have a job that I enjoy and that gives me time to spend with friends and family. And even though we recently lost my mother, she was able to pass without having the dementia she saw her mother struggle through that she always feared.

So. these are the things I am grateful for. These things, though simple to some, are things that I never thought possible. Meister Eckhart once said, according to Brainy Quotes, "If the only prayer you ever say in your entire life is thank you, it will be enough". I tend to agree. Though I did not know his advice prior to my starting each prayer that way. I am grateful for so many things throughout the day. There are so many things that happen that benefit me and protect me which happen unaware, that I do not know all for what to be thankful. May we all find a peace that allows us to be grateful. And as a side note, please be aware, that when things seem bleak, there are always others, who when they say thank you to the Creator for "everything", are including you as one of the things for which they give thanks.

The Wisers

I saw an old photograph tonight. It took me back to a time when things were more certain, more innocent, and more wholesome. They were good times. They were the times in my life when I had a firm belief that my conscience was useful and something I could act on, that there was good to be done in the world and my only obligation was to discover it, that the friends I had made would be lifelong companions. During this time and place in my life, there were the Wisers.

Norah was kind and a great teacher. Bill was quiet and was great at getting things done. Together they were the youth directors of my childhood church. Together, they were the goal of what I tried to achieve in my years as a youth minister. As far as I know, they were "part time" with the church, though you never suspected they did anything other than love on kids. I think Norah may have been the church secretary and Bill was a fireman. They may be surprised to know the effect they had on so many lives, but I would not. They had a great effect on mine and still do.

Bill drove the big, yellow, church bus. We would stop and he would get out and light a cigarette. A cigarette I am sure he needed after hauling around a bunch of teenagers. He took us to New York, to the beach, and many other places. One night in the dormitory style beach house we were staying in, some of my friends decided to fly a Frisbee that glowed in the dark to all our other friends in the top bunks. I was so excited when someone finally threw it to me. I was more excited that I caught it. At that moment, that very instant, before I could determine who to throw it to next, Bill Wiser, out of nowhere, in a deep soft voice, spoke directly in my ear, "Put it down and go to sleep".

I did just that. He never said another word about it and I never thought he was mad. In retrospect, that seemed like the perfect reaction for a youth director. One that even God might have if he thought I was doing wrong. But the funny thing about the Wisers was this. They never tried to convince me to believe anything. They never did anything but love me. They never crammed anything down my proverbial throat. Yet, because of that, when I think of them, I remember good times, but I am also compelled to do good for others, as they did good to me and countless others. And that seems to be the gospel, doesn't it? The Wisers did not teach me about Jesus, they taught me, by their example, to be Jesus.

I fail to do it daily, but I think nothing would be better, than to live what I learned in a church office, or in a top bunk, or even getting off of a big, yellow, bus.

To Be a Memory

Sometimes I wonder how I will be remembered. Sometimes I wonder how I am remembered now. It occurs to me, that if I am remembered at all, the man I gave a sandwich to on the corner of Cumberland has a different memory of me than, for example, an ex-girlfriend, a former teacher, or college friend. Memories are so informed by the person with the memory. I have been cursed and I have been praised, on occasion, by the same person.

And while each new day brings different people into my life and an opportunity to "create a new me", often, I tend to want to stay in bed or be alone, so as not to do more harm than good. Ultimately, it is not my image that I worry so much about. I would like to think that I represent the Divine. I hope that when others encounter me, they might be compelled to think about, in some small way, God. This is a responsibility that I take on myself, but one that has always been a part of my concern, at least in the back of my mind, if not some sort of mission.

I was never impressed with the "WWJD" (What Would Jesus Do?) campaign. It may be important to some and might have helped others, but for me, the constant question is, "WSKD" (What Should Kevin Do?). Generally, I do not ask myself that question enough. Generally, I make decisions and hope for the best. I would like to think that I was informed in my decision making by what Jesus did and does on earth, but when it comes down to it, there is nothing written about Jesus having to hold for an hour and a half to convince someone on the other end of a telephone line that he was billed incorrectly on his utility bill. Hopefully, there are more options to handling things than one divinely ordained response.

So, what can I do about how I am remembered? What great advice could I take so as not to do damage to the kingdom? I have heard, "Love One Another". If that is not possible for some, and on some days for me I cannot do it well, here is the advice I try to follow. "Don't be a jerk". It is hard sometimes. It is hard for me a lot of times. But it follows the thinking that if you cannot do good, at least, do no harm. It may not bring some great reward, but I have found I sleep better when I got through a day without acting mean. Of course, I prefer love, but the absence of meanness will suffice.

As far as being a memory? I find that even those I felt negatively about years ago have become, to some extent, endeared to me when I remember them. Some of the most painful memories I have had found a way of losing their sting with the passing of time. So, I live, hopefully without the pressure of the kingdom of God resting on my shoulders alone. Hopefully, without being responsible for every person's opinion of me. And hopefully, even still, knowing that there is a grace for anything I could do wrong, a mercy for every action I could set into motion, and a forgiveness for every transgression I could perform. This is peace. This is how I would like to be remembered.

Current Resident

There is something to be said about having a home. There is something to be said about having friends and family around as you venture out into the world each day. Likewise, there is some comfort in having a place where you might worship. Some comfort in gathering with like-minded people working towards a worthy cause. What these things said, or comforts are in particular, could be debated until the proverbial cows come home.

What is it then, that can be said about not having such things? While I have never been homeless, I have spent time, on occasion, nights, with people living on the street. There have been times when I could not take solace in friendship. I have no physical place to worship and though I am a free mason, my contribution to our charitable causes are mostly in the form of monetary gifts (and even that embarrassingly little). Even though I have more than I deserve, I have some understanding of what it is to have little. Most of us are in the same boat.

Most of life is an illusion. It is created by what we have been taught, by what we have decided to value, and by our impression that things, beliefs, and even beauty are permanent. And if I may, God, in some sense, is an illusion. Rather, our impression of God, if we strive to learn more of the Divine each day, is an illusion. For example, I have been me for 48 years. The six-year old me is different from the me I was at age twenty-one, which is different from the me I am today. And quite frankly, I am not even sure I understand the present me completely. So, homes, the lack of homes, friends, the lack of friends, houses of worship, the absence of those houses, and groups, or the lack of groups, are in essence, an illusion at most, and not permanent at least.

My advice is simple, but it helps some people. Shut your eyes and all that you see is yours. In turn, all that you do not see is yours as well. The Creator exists in all of creation. The Divine passes through you and you through the Divine. In some respects, it is up to you to only be absorbed into the One who dwells in you already. I would recommend not worrying so much about the will of God for your life, but if the direction you are heading in is in the flow of what God is doing in the world today. Do not reject the things you own or enjoy, but always have a healthy suspicion about how they shape your opinion of others or of God.

Be responsible. Be kind. Be joyful. Be love to one another. Be peace. Be happy. Be excited. Be limited by only what you can see, or cannot see, with your eyes closed. Your beginning was known before you came to earth and your end is non-existent. This eternal life that some speak of starts now, not after we die. The Universe knows you and chose you. You have made it this far. That is a big deal. As for our situation now, this is not our home, we are all, each one, but a current resident.

You Do You

For all intents and purposes, my life, both long and short in comparison to others, should be over by now. Somewhat due to the decisions I have made and somewhat due to what has been thrust upon me by the universe. Even though, honestly, at times it is hard for me to distinguish the difference between the two. As I sit now, only a few things are certain. The new day is a gift. Each breath is unexpected. And there are more things for me to accomplish that what has been done prior to the situation I find myself in now.

My goal is not to buy the world a soda or have them sing in some harmonious chorus, perfectly. My goal is not to have each human on earth bow to one god or another. My goal is certainly not to have people that I meet conform to my understanding of a deity or my particular belief system. People, and their ideas of God and the world, are different. I am alright with that. Like it or not, I believe that God is aright with that as well. If any one person had a complete grasp of the Universe, there would be nothing left to learn, and I would imagine both that person, and the Universe, would become quite bored and disinterested in one another.

In our American world, I would explain God like this. As an example, taken from my kitchen. Though I do not understand electricity, it is there. If I want coffee, I plug in a coffee pot to an outlet. If I want toast, I plug in the toaster. If I want, and I rarely do, a healthy smoothie, I plug in a blender. Of course, the same source of electricity provides power for a dishwasher, refrigerator/freezer, cell phone charger, microwave, and whatever other device that I might deem handy at the time. Same electricity, different appliances, different purposes served.

There is a cost for the electricity. Both for the power and the outlets. The privilege of receiving electricity has to be earned by someone. I know not to stick a fork in the outlets. Electricity, while helpful, can also be dangerous if it is misused. There is one source for the power in my kitchen. It is up to the people who wired the outlets to decide how much goes where and it is up to me to choose the right appliance for whichever need I have at the moment. One thing I might also add is, like God's favor, people never seem to miss it until it is not there. Most don't come in, turn their lights on and say, "Awesome!!! I can see!!!".

As for my original thought, as to there being more for me to accomplish, I would like for every coffee not to be made to feel like it is responsible for keeping the lettuce and milk cold. I would like for a toaster not to be made to feel that if the dishes do not get clean, that it is somehow responsible. We are all an appliance of some sort, having to be plugged in to the Divine, to be used by the Divine. If you are made to make coffee, do not long to make toast. And for the sake of everyone involved, do not set up a list of rules and organizations that claim only coffee makers have access to the power of electricity and that coffee is the favored beverage and function of the Creator.

I suppose I have just written a parable about objects that are not animated, which Jesus would not do because his audience was not accustomed to harnessed electricity. I suppose my point here is, marvel at the intricacies of a phone charger even if you are a garbage disposal. And if you are a blender, do not worry yourself with making toast. Be content with having power to do what you do.

Enjoy the day, the breath, and accomplish something worthwhile. You are loved. You have more strength than you know. You are connected directly to the source of all that powers the entire Universe. And though you could be better (as could we all), you are fine right now.

To Speak of Things

It seems odd that the very validity of words would be questioned. Odd that information, that the internet is packed with, would be called into suspicion. That something written in English, the world's second language, would disparage the holding of one language in higher regard than another. And it is odd, that as I sit in my climate-controlled home, in the fall, near the Appalachian Mountains, drinking a clean, caffeinated drink, that I would call what most call, blessings, a distraction.

There are so many things that bombard us each day. Some we choose, some we do not. Some use information to heal, some for destruction, a lot for promotion or personal gain. It makes us feel good momentarily if we "know" something others may not. It helps us connect to others that "know" the same thing. It makes us feel even better if we can share what we know with someone that may not know. In truth, we know very little about so few things. It is not a conspiracy theory, but the transmission of truth has become so lazily done as of late, that not much is being done to educate, while much more is being done to "look" educated.

Words, good or bad, have a way of developing power. They have inspired, they have destroyed, they have created smiles, and they have initiated despair. The one thing they have in common is, that the power they have to do these things, is given by the those that perceive them. A word as simple as "go" may be heard by someone who is comfortable where they are as a burden. For someone who is unhappy with their situation, the word "go" may be salvation. Same word, different perceptions.

Without a discussion of linguistics or political involvement, the point needs to be made that English, though the dominant language in the world today, for whatever reason, may not be the favored language of the Divine. One may not need to know Hebrew, though it was used to write the sacred text for Judaism, to enter the gates of Heaven. Arabic, though it is beautifully written, may not be the only language there is to perceive the will of God. I think the Creator cares about as much about I Phone/Android debates or the early IBM/Apple debates as he does about which languages are used.

Somewhere along the way, we as humanity, have been tricked into thinking that information is truth. We are convinced, as humanity, that there is a First World and a Third World (I always wondered where the Second World was). While I commend people from the United States for traveling to less economically rich countries to "minister", I wonder why they don't simply use the money it takes to go abroad to bring others here to preach. Though many preachers have become rich saying otherwise, having a coffee maker or fancy car has little to do with God and everything to do with the world.

Where does that leave us? Did not the Creator "speak" the world into existence? Is not Christ, according to the Gospel, the "Word of God"? Though some may claim heresy, and some may say I have missed the point, I tell you, there is more truth in helping someone from the ground, with a bag of groceries, or in a compassionate smile, than there is in all of the volumes of Sacred Texts that can be read. And certainly, more truth in a small act of kindness, like looking into the eyes of a man or woman found homeless, rather than speeding one's step as they walk by, than anything heard on CNN or read in USA Today. All without words. All manifesting the love of God. All without money. And all, building a world of which not only the Divine, but we as humans, can be proud.

Fitting In

There are times in my life, as I am sure there are times in many lives, that I feel separated from others and what is going on in this world. If I were truthful, I would have to admit that most of my days have been spent wondering where I belong and without much zeal or conviction about one subject or another. While I have beliefs that are similar to beliefs of particular groups of people, I also have the experience and knowledge that most of those beliefs have evolved, if not changed, over time.

Maybe it is that I am too critical. It may be that I am so uncomfortable with my own thoughts, that if others have them also, I question their validity. And perhaps, it is my opinion that all things, thoughts, beliefs, friends, authorities, beauty, and even love, fade like a setting sun into a dark night sky, void of anything that was visible before dusk. And at some point, it is the guilt I feel over having life easier and with more abundance than others that I know exist in the world. With that said, I am certain I do not fit in with many circles or groups.

Bleak? Could be. Burdensome? Could be. Overwhelming and hopeless? Not at all. While I do not know what purpose that I might serve in life, or even what point there is to it all, there is a steady rhythm beating in the day to day. It sounds with every beat of my heart. It lives with every breath I take. The world is different, be it for the better or for the worse, because I am in it. That is the group I fit into. The group that all of humanity finds itself. We all, by virtue of our waking, make a difference. There is no neutral in the way we live or think. So, when possible, these are the things I try to accomplish each day.

Make someone smile. Speak to one stranger a day. Tell my family "I love you". Say one nice thing to someone about someone else. Pray. Read, even if it is only a quote. Think. Be purposefully grateful. And realize that most, if not all, of what I do is a choice.

And here is the good news. If you find that you cannot do these things in real time, do them in your mind in your free time. Doing a kind deed in thought will reap the same benefit as doing a kind deed in the world. I may not fit in. I may not be well known. I may not become influential or have great power. But I will, without reservation, love with the same passion, grace, and fervor, as the Creator has shown to me. Hopefully, even when they put ketchup on my hamburger when I specifically told them to hold it.

Piano Woman

Many years ago, when things seemed more certain, or at least more clear-cut, I was invited to join a team of basketball players who would double as missionaries during a trip to Zambia. We were good enough at basketball to play exhibition games around the country against the Zambian National Team and we came from far away enough that people were intrigued with what we had to say about God. My father always said, with regard to building materials, that if you were from more than 30 miles away from the problem, you were the expert. We stayed overseas around a month and the trip was paid for by donations to the then Baptist Student Union at the University of Tennessee.

One of the requirements after being selected for the team was to provide the BSU with a list of friends and family who might be willing to donate to the trip. My family came through. My friends came through. My church at the time came through. There was very little out of pocket expense for me and I will always be grateful for those who made it possible. When word spread around my relatively small church that I was going to Africa and that I was raising money, a lady I barely knew, but that had watched me grow up, made an offer to my mother. Though she had no extra money, she wanted to offer me piano lessons at no cost, for as long as I would like.

At first, being busy with my studies, and being busier with things other than my studies, I wanted to decline. My mother insisted I take lessons, not because she wanted me to play piano, but because her friend had offered to give me the lessons. So off I went to the church where I had grown up. Sitting in the sanctuary where I was baptized, where I first questioned what it was that

God wanted from me, where, even as Southern Baptist as the lessons were, I began learning about the Divine. I knew very little about the piano and I knew even less about this woman that was kind enough to teach me some new skill.

This story would be awesome if it ended with a great friendship that was formed. Greater even still, if I could say that every time, I play some great work from some great composer that I think of my teacher from so many years ago. The truth is, without my mother here, I can seldom remember the lady's name and I cannot play piano. I do not know what she did for the church. I do not know what she did for a living. I do not know how, her and my mother met, and I do not know what her particular beliefs were on any small or great matter that everyone concerns themselves with today.

What I do remember is her smile. I remember her patience. I remember her calm and gentle spirit. And I remember her gift to me. Lessons that lasted for however long and were given for however many weeks or months.

Sometimes what we give may not seem like so very much to others and it might not even meet the need of the request. It may also be of note that it was good for her to be able to teach me, in some small way. That we may have been a blessing to each other. As for the trip to the nation of Zambia, the team was 4-0, we saw some really cool things, great times, met some good people, and we got home safe. Thanks to all the donors and "The Piano Woman". Happy Saturday.

Milestones

As in everyone's life, there are times that I remember from my childhood, that I can go back to in my mind, where memories seem as real as the air I breathe today. Where the feelings and thoughts I had in the past come over me with the same sense of urgency, hope, fear, elation, dread, and joy. There were five minutes of my life as a second or third grader, where I was near death (in my mind), that shape every interaction I have with school age children. Five minutes of a panic, running home from school, that only a young child can have.

It all goes back to the introduction of one of the all-time coolest inventions ever to hit a school classroom. The Sta-Sharp pencil. It was a plastic tube full of sharp pencil lead points glued into small plastic backings. After one point became dull or broke, one could simply remove it from the bottom of the tube and press it into the top of the tube and a new sharp point appeared. In all honesty, I do not know how many points were in a complete pencil, because after a few uses, it became apparent that the design was much more conducive to adaptation for shooting spit balls at classmates.

To improve on the spit ball variation of the invention, my friends and I started shooting the actual pencil leads at one another through the tube. The projectiles were sharp and heavier. It made perfect sense. My five minutes of dying came, not from being hit with one of the leads, but from a misfire on the pencil. On the way home, and after taking aim at an older kid, I inhaled a deep breath while getting ready to take a shot and breathed in a pencil lead. I did not choke, I did not gasp, but it dawned on me that I would get what I had heard of, even as a child, "lead poisoning". My only thought was how fast I could run home to see my mother before I died.

I am able to walk those streets today and if I tried, I might possibly even be able to run the same route. Those streets will not, however, lead me to my mother. There were many times in my life, though not in a panic over dying, that I ran home to my mother as quickly as I could. Just to be hugged and to get an explanation that everything I have heard about, like lead poisoning, might not be true. I find myself these days, since she has passed, running towards her, not with speed in mind, but with wanting to finish well. Knowing that one day we will embrace again and knowing that while her race is run, there is still a journey for me to travel. One mile at a time.

One Note

When I was younger and had time that seems to escape me now, I would go down to The Strip and hang out in bars where I would play a little pool and foosball. I enjoyed the people there, but what I liked most was hanging out with the musicians playing in the streets for tips. Say what you want about that lifestyle. Criticize the element with which I was surrounding myself. Feel better about the way you live as opposed to the lives they were living if it gives you some sense of satisfaction. There were life lessons there being taught on those streets. Often times with no inclination that class was in session.

Sitting cross legged (another thing I cannot do today) next to a man and his dog, admiring the way he played the blues, I saw and heard a college student walk by and mutter something ugly to his friends. I looked at this man with a guitar in his hand after he had finished his song and asked if he had heard what the young guy had said as he passed. He never answered my question but said, without a second thought, "A whole universe of darkness can be overcome by one spark".

As I tend to do, I thought about this great advice and wisdom for a full week. When I saw the blues man and his dog the following Saturday, I started a conversation that would allow him to elaborate on what he had obviously taken years to develop as a life philosophy. He did not remember saying anything remotely similar to what I had adopted as a great teaching. He must have been drunk, he said. He must have been drunk. Drunk or not, it is still something I think about to this day.

While on topic of the universe, guitars, and listening to music, I would like to offer some advice of my own. The universe creates a song each day. There are many who hear it for what it is, there are many who believe it is their own, and there are many who, for good or for bad, have forgotten how to hear the music. Our actions and intentions create one note. We may never get the chance to hear the one note another in Zimbabwe created or get a chance to share our note with a Brazilian, but we are one, indispensable, hopefully beautiful, song.

The notes we create are sung by God to the world as a whole. I want to believe the title is "Love One Another", but you might believe it is something different. We are a note in the song, yet we are not the song. We create a note in the song but have not created the song. It can be sung only by the Divine. As for those who cannot hear the tune anymore? They can be a "rest" on the music sheet, just as important as any note.

We are writing the music for God to sing. I hope we remember what he requested the song be about. I hope it is good enough to be performed. I hope we have not lost our ability to sing it alongside the Creator to help creation. In case you ever wondered about yourself, even though you might be a little off sometimes, never doubt that you are a good note. One note worth singing. One note worth hearing. Welcome to the band.

Hope is Hard

For what do we hope? What do we expect out of the uncertain times that we live in? Have we become numb to the endless possibilities that exist in a world where every need is either immediately satisfied or discarded as not worth the effort? In a world that gives us Facebook instead of friends, fast food instead of meals, memes instead of discussions, and immediate religious answers rather than a passion for learning about God, it is difficult to have something as simple, yet as courageous, as hope.

Hope is not a Christmas list. Hope is not what you want on our birthdays. Hope is something constant and eternal. Something that lasts and that is created in us each day. Hope is something we may possess but is not something we create in ourselves. We are given hope by others and by the Eternal, and can only, at any given point in time, receive more by giving it to others. Hope may be the only thing that keeps us hanging on and it may be the only thing we are able to gift to another person. It does not cost anything to have and it costs nothing to give away. We can have as much as we like, but it is something to be shared.

I have heard it said that "my cup runs over". To that I say, as I have heard taught in Kabbalah, get a different cup. We can be full of hope and compassion without our cup running over. If we take the bottom out of our cup and place it under the ever-flowing fountain of hope and compassion, we become a conduit. Ever flowing into the top and ever flowing out of bottom. So, it is great if those around you receive what has flown over the top of your cup, but it is better if they are blessed by the same thing, and at the same rate, as you were so fortunate to be blessed. Hope will never run dry if we receive it. It will never run dry if we give it away. It will never be never.

Hope is not an attitude. Hope is, believe it or not, a real thing. It is a trust in something higher and more knowing, than we are now. As with anything or anybody, it takes time to build trust. It is evident in the smile of a homeless woman, in the hug of a small child in poverty, in a parent that wants more for his or her teenage son or daughter, and even in a flower blooming in the snow. Hope is an understanding and a way of life. Hope is knowing that no matter how bad a situation seems, there is a lesson to be learned and a better day coming.

So here I am writing about hope. Thinking there is something I can say that has not been said a million times before. My purpose here is not to come up with some great new discourse on hope. My purpose is to let you know that there is a reason for hope. That if you have a little hope today, it will grow into a larger hope tomorrow. The secret to holding hope is to know that what you are seeing is only about ten percent of what is real in this world. And of that ten percent, your perception of things is one in seven billion. Hold on to hope and know that others care. And though hope is hard, it is based on one simple eternal truth. Something bigger *than* you, wants something bigger *for* you.

Killing the Sacred

Humanity is weird sometimes. We cling to objects in hopes that they might bring us closer to the divine, all with fervor and passion, and most times, with a willingness to sacrifice relationships and even the lives of others and ourselves. There is not much to say here, other than the relationships, our lives, and others, are often the only things that were sacred from the beginning.

Sacred texts have become such an issue around the world. One group holds a text as sacred while another group holds a different text in high regard. It would be more convincing to me that a text was sacred if the ones that viewed it as such did not gain a substantial income from the publishing of what they deem necessary for others to come into contact with the divine. What is the going rate for what you would consider "The Word of God"?

Holy places would be worth a pilgrimage if there had not been bloody battles fought over, in, and around the areas, devotees claim, are sacred. Temples, mosques, churches, synagogues, sanctuaries, and worship centers have all become, for at least one hour of the week, the most segregated places in the world. Often times, the messages taught in these "holy places" are divisive and self-congratulatory. And in America, most resemble a country club or fitness center, where members only are allowed to utilize the facilities.

Most clergy, clerics, TV evangelists, preachers, and religious teachers are paid. It lies in their best interest not to offend their constituency. Some well, some not. There are good men and women espousing their beliefs and there are some that "spoil the bushel". For every kind heart found in a member of religious leadership there are ten hearts filled with something other than the love of God. There are three major religions that profess the sovereignty of one God and there are thousands of different versions of those religions who think they are the only ones who are theologically correct.

So, if it ever did exist, we have killed the sacred. We continue killing the sacred every day. The good news? There are billions of sacred places in the world yet undiscovered. Simply put, there is a place in each of us that only God can dwell. Not with our thoughts, not with our emotions or devotion, and not with our beliefs. Only God can exist there, and that place is found within us. So, while wars rage, debates fly about, and teachers teach "the truth", God dwells quietly in us. And for the record, you must be one special somebody for that to happen. May we bear the weight of the responsibility that brings.

It Matters

In every life, at some point it seems, a question comes about that asks if any of this really matters. Anyone with any sense can see the world, as it is, and wonder what sense any of it makes. From one world view to the next, from one natural disaster to the next, from one war to the next, we cannot help but to question if there is a purpose to anything, we as individuals, do in and for this world. While I may not know the meaning of life, I do have three secrets, though they are not secrets, at all, that may help navigate the sense of meaninglessness one might, on occasion, feel.

First, dial it in. Realize the scope of your responsibility. If one watches the news and sees a skirmish in Zimbabwe, or a drought in an area that is unknown, or a group of humans acting ill toward another group of humans, learn from it and let it go. It may pass as compassion to obsess over whatever the media spoon feeds you, but unless you are committed to a cause and are doing something proactive to help, there is no need for worry, discourse, or this or that opinion on the matter. And if you need a reason not to fret, realize that God has more troops on the ground than you have and that He is, ultimately, in control.

Second, be grateful. Not grateful in the sense that at least we have it better than others, but grateful that in this moment our needs are met. Not grateful that things will get better, but that in this moment, we are surviving. Not grateful that it will all make sense someday, because in truth, it may never make sense. And not grateful that one day there will be a heaven for us and the ones we love, because this is the Kingdom of God and the ones who passed into heaven do not typically come back with reports on that which we have to look forward. But, be grateful for the fact that you are here. And realize that in this moment, all the potential for joy, peace, and meaning, exists within you. Right now.

Third, keep secrets. In this age of social media and our propensity to telling everything we know, it is hard to keep a secret. I am not talking about cheating on your boyfriend or girlfriend and not telling them. I am not talking about bumping a car in the parking lot and not leaving a note. Do good things. Do good things and don't let anyone know. Do good things for people, groups, even yourself, and do not let anyone be the wiser. It helps create a sense in oneself that, though no one was told, that a good deed is known. And honestly, our attitude changes when we have a secret with the universe. When we release a good deed with the telling of it, we release the good deed, and honestly, it does us little good afterward.

What I know is this. Except to humanity, religion, race, creed, and nationality, means absolutely nothing to the Creator. And though this seems like a heretical parable, if a single mother has seven kids from seven fathers, she is not likely to love one more or less because of where the child came from. Likewise, the Creator loves us all. If we cannot be kind to one another, at least let us not incite hatred. If we cannot have compassion, at least let us not cause pain. And if we cannot help our neighbors up, at least let us not kick them when they are down. Why, you ask? Because it matters.

The Secret Word of Power

If you are going to read this blog entry, please read to the end. There is a secret for all of humanity found in these words. There is a challenge for those that might offer relief or help to others. And finally, there is a confronting of old ideas and a truth that only ancient mystics know. Those that know me, know more of Sha-Pow than others, and will see the truth in the following words, being made known, only at the end of this blog.

In ancient Tibet, when warriors trained for battle, there were levels of training to be attained. When each of seventeen levels was attained, a secret word was given to the soldier who completed the training, that would release a power which made weapons stronger, the mind more focused, and opponents as weak as "the rivers that flow to the sea". When the seventeenth, and final word was given, and the master soldier was sworn to secrecy, he (very few females studied this art in ancient times, though this secret is for all humanity now), was given this word.

There was only one written record of the word discussed through oral tradition and it was passed down to each of the many Dalai Lamas through his incarnations. The current Dalai Lama, thinking he was not being recorded, as portable recording devices were in their infancy stage of development, passed this word to a student in the early 1940's. This recording surfaced in 1982 and has changed the world of those who recite it, in all facets of their lives. When repeated in meditations at least ten minutes in the morning and ten minutes before sleep, the word brings peace, purpose, and attracts all the help the Universe has to offer the one who births the word into the world.

Because I care for you. Because I take my readers interests as a cause for my incantations of the word. Because the world needs more peace, purpose, and help from the universe. I am sharing this word with you. The word is Sha-Pow. In the last two decades of my life I have followed the secret ways of meditating on the word meant only for the elite, and my life has improved in many ways. My savings account has increased more than 100-fold, my relationships have become harmonious, and the fungus I had under my left big toe nail has all but left. I have manifested running, clean, water into my kitchen almost every morning before making coffee. When my children pass gas, there are glitter filled rainbows that light the room.

All this because of "Sha-Pow".

Actually, I have been saying Sha-Pow with excitement since my early twenties. It is a word I made up when playing foosball and used to emphasize things that some people might use "booyah" for, today. I have been watching people for nearly fifty years. I have paid some attention to religions and religious people for some time, as well. Recently, I have been listening to positive thought literature and also watching documentaries on cults. People are gullible. I believe God is good, that God is a giving god, and that we need to learn to *receive* more than we need to learn to *ask* more. My general rule is this. Good news shared is great. Good news that can only be accessed through a leader, a process, a religious organization, or one particular text, is as crooked as granddad's walking stick… that stick was crooked as all get out.

It costs nothing to think positively. It costs nothing to smile. Can we attract things with our minds that make us happy? I hope not. I hope we use our minds to create happiness, and not things. Joy is not traded on Wall Street, but books on happiness are peddled in every bookstore and on every book website. Here is my recommendation for instant happiness (nothing to do with Sha-Pow). Be grateful. Then get on YouTube and put the Bobby McFerrin video of "Don't Worry Be Happy" on a loop. Play it for hours at a time. You will either be happy afterwards because it inspired you, or you will be happy it is finally not playing in your ear. Either way, be grateful again.

Receive what the Divine has to offer. Do not receive what the Divine gave another and is being offered for resale. As far as Sha-Pow goes, use that one for free. That one's on the house.

A Station in Life

As a college student, on spring break, I traveled with a group of peers to Miami. We worked in a mission there for a week. For some reason, I was asked to speak to the clients of the mission on a Sunday morning. It was a large audience and they were captive, literally, as they had to endure a "service" before they could eat breakfast that day. My only question was, "What could a middleclass college kid say to people living on the streets of a town that seemed a million miles away from where I grew up?".

My answer came from my favorite professor, Dr. Dungan, who suggested speaking about the widow that was so persistent that her needs were eventually met.

So, I spoke of those things, trying to encourage these men and women to not lose hope, to keep trying, to not give up. Not give up struggling for whatever they were working towards. Not give up on God. Or humanity. It lasted a good fifteen minutes, and when it was over, I went into the bathroom and cried. I felt I had done little for anyone that day. I wanted to believe my tears came from a place inside me that was empathetic or filled with compassion. In truth, my tears came from not being able to better the lives of the people I was "helping" instantly, which was, a direct contradiction, to the advice I had just delivered.

Like it or not, fair or not, we all start at some point with a station, or place, in life. It is ignorant to believe that there is no privilege, or racism, or elitism in the world. We are where we are, most likely, because of some system of preference or some preference given by someone. It is important to recognize this. It is heresy to believe it is ordained or created by God. There are those who work their way up and there are those who allow themselves to fall. Our station is, of course, man made, but it is also, of course, a manmade reality. What then can we do to help others? Honestly, I have no ideas on the matter. Perhaps we should wake each day with a desire to help where we can, to start. If we get crazy, we might believe peace is possible.

A couple of years after this experience, I wrote a song. Some of which is shared below.

"Living ain't worth living, unless you're into dying. Dying ain't worth dying, 'til you've lived.

Giving ain't worth giving, unless you're into taking. Taking ain't worth taking, 'til you give.

Pray for Love, live to see its face. Make your home, in the light of its embrace.

Life is short, and our days they are not long. You gotta do what you can, to help the world along."

The Man Who Raised Me

My father is, and was, many things, to many people. He speaks less than he listens. He learns more than he teaches. He gives more to others than he spends on himself. He worked for the same company for 50 years and he was married to my mother for more than those before her death just over a year ago. He is a free mason, a Southern Baptist Sunday School teacher, a modern-day thinker and an observer of traditions. He was a Kentucky Colonel, an airplane pilot, an avid golfer, a bowler, a part time mechanic, one who tinkers, and with all of these things going on, always had time to kick a ball back and forth with me in the yard.

There are a million stories I could share about the man who raised me (and in truth, is still raising me at age 48). A million ways he has supported me, shared my visions, or counselled me on various matters involving personal gains or losses. One summer we dug a 3-feet by 10-feet hole in the ground, by hand, 18 feet deep, because I thought we might hit water. When I decided to live in Virginia for three summers or spend a month in Africa, he simply asked if I thought it was a good idea and what I would need. He listened to me ramble about my first love as if it was the only real thing in life and he listened to my stories of heartache when many loves afterward failed to last. He has pursued me when I needed to be caught and has let me go in love when I needed to be free.

I can still hear his words on an Easter Sunday in my mid-twenties. He had arrived home from church to find me waiting in the driveway. It was after my divorce and there was something about church that did not appeal to me that particular day. We spoke about the service at his church and I explained, most likely more to myself than to him, the various reasons I did not attend a service that day. "Dad, it is Easter Sunday and I didn't go to church. Should I feel bad?". His response was simply, "It is still Easter, isn't it?".

Those words have guided my life, though he may not even remember the conversation. When I am tempted to worry, criticize a situation, or agonize over the past, I am reminded that no matter my involvement, God is at work. And in the same vein, if we are tempted to believe our critics when they doubt our ability or beauty, we are still crafted by the Creator, aren't we? There have been many Sundays since that conversation that I have not attended a church service and the world did not end. What I can say about my lack of pew time is that I have learned more about life, God, and myself, not from attending a service or reading a text, but from the man who raised me.

Life Is Not a Miracle

Life is not a miracle. Life is one of the most common things a person could see if one took the time to look around. A flower has life. A butterfly has life. Even the water we drink, though tough to think about, is teaming with life. No, life is not a miracle, but living life, now that is a miraculous thing indeed. Perhaps I am not so impressed with the miracle of life because I have never participated in the creation myself. Perhaps because I have no biological children, I am desensitized to what a wonder it is.

Living is what intrigues me. What we do with something as common as life in order to help others create something as common as life. There is constant motion in this world. Even as we sleep, something is happening around the globe, and even, in our own bodies. For those of us who take seriously the admonition to "be still, and know that I am God", it is understood that we are not simply to "be still", but also to "know". In us creation is created, and through us, we create creation. It is kind of a big deal. An honor, if you will.

So, what have I made with this creation in me if I have not created children of my own? What have I done that is worthy of the honor of which I have been bestowed? It is not money. Though I have made money, it is not worthy of that honor. It is not time. Time is an illusion that slips through your fingers like, well, the sands of time. It is not art or music, as noble as those are. Sometimes, even though I do make a mess, I create things of which I am proud.

My finest achievements? I may not have made a baby, but I have made fine young men and women. They are my children. Some may call them my step kids, my nieces, or my nephews, but I call them all my own. I have made friends. Some through work, some through bars, some through church, but my friends, none the less. I have made love. Not always in the sexual sense, but in the way my wife and I live with each other, the way I treat strangers as well as my family, and the way I try to take the grace that has been afforded me and give the same grace to those I meet.

This is the miracle of living for me. You may do living differently. But when it feels like you cannot go on, "be still, and know that I am God". And if that is not possible, be still and know that someone has been there before you and they care more for you than you can see at the time. No one has living figured out. They simply have figured out how to give the impression that living is easy. And please, for the love of all that is holy in this world and the next, understand that you are the real miracle and the true love of the Creator. And that, my friends, is a big deal.

Papaw Party

Michelle called him Barty. Their relationship was complicated, as Michelle's parents were divorced while she was new to the world. I've heard stories. Some good. Some bad. When I met him, he was confined to a bed. Paralyzed from the neck down after a fall from a balcony. Twenty years prior the doctors gave him five years, at most, to live. We went to his house so Michelle could cut his very long hair.

His new wife was not home, and he was lying there, playing video games with some tool that allowed him control with his head. His smile was contagious and his commentary on life in general was refreshing. No matter what had happened in the past and no matter how he had gotten to where he was, I couldn't help but like him. I held his head while Michelle cut the back. And then, I fell in love with Michelle even more deeply as she asked Barty if he wanted a cigarette. I smoked then, she never did.

She put a cigarette into a loop of iron fastened to his wristband and lit it. It was apparent that he enjoyed it and I wondered how long he had been there just wanting to smoke. There were other brief visits and eventually he found himself in the hospital for the last time. Though I have known people, including my mother, that have died, he is the only person I have been with when they passed.

Mostly for Michelle, but for him as well. He was my wife's father, yet somehow, in the brief time that I knew him, he became my friend. I remember one thing more than others about Barty.

Maybe to others, but never to me, did he once complain about his situation. He laughed when we spoke. He cut up with me when we talked. His family loved him. Perhaps I saw only one side of Barty. Perhaps my memory is skewed. But I remember a kind man, with a sharp mind, a wonderful sense of humor, and a great will to survive. At his funeral, Michelle, in her children's honor, placed a pillow inside his casket that read, "Papaw Party". The name they called him when they were young. And though this may seem odd, I was happy that my mother, upon her passing, was able to meet the man. I am a better person for meeting the man myself. May we be thankful for what we have, who we have, and the time we have to enjoy them.

Your Buddy and Your Bike

Just after my first marriage began, thoughts of riding a motorcycle entered my mind. I took a class. I got my license. I bought a used Kawasaki. I rode it home and parked it in an old wood garage outside of a two-bedroom farm house we rented for $300/month. The farm house was just off a road in West Knoxville that had not yet been consumed by the half million-dollar homes that would eventually be planted there. It was a dead-end road and was perfect for gatherings of friends.

At one of these gatherings, one of these friends said, "Can I take your motorcycle the end of the road and back?"

My response was quick. I assured him that it would be fine with me, and it was. Down the road he rode as I listened to the motor's pitch change with each shift of the gears. Before he returned, a silence fell on the road. We all came to the conclusion that he had stopped to talk to one of the neighbors and we went on with dinner. After a while, he came walking beside the motorcycle, with a worried and concerned look on his face. He crashed but was alright, though the motorcycle was not.

A few days later, I called another friend who had ridden for years. He came over and helped me fix my motorcycle. As we talked about what happened, he looked up at me and said, "Kevin, never let your buddy ride your bike."

Immediately after that wisdom was shared, he sat on the seat of my motorcycle, started the engine, pointed to his motorcycle as if to tell me to hop onto it, and we rode to the mountains. When we traded rides in the mountains to go our separate ways, he never said a word about his previous statement. He just smiled and we rode back to Knoxville. There was his admonition, then there was his trust.

So, it is with God. No matter how many times I have crashed, no matter how many times I have violated this or that law of the universe, no matter what destruction or damage I have left in my wake, God comes to where I am, helps repair the things that are in disarray, and gives me, of all things, trust. He trusts humanity, and you and I in particular, with not only executing His plan, but with creating His will. If this seems blasphemous, consider why we pray or petition God to do anything on behalf of others or ourselves. And as far as letting your buddy ride your bike? Let your buddy find his own ride. It is for you to live the life you have. But if at some point, you counted on someone to make you happy, on some material thing to give you joy, or on some job to give you meaning, God will get you back on the road.

Two Burdens, One Joy

In the early nineties, there was an old woman sitting by the road I was traveling towards Lusaka, Zambia. She sat there, every day, for the better part of the day, making smaller rocks out of bigger rocks with a chisel and hammer. As I walked by in my shorts and short sleeves, looking as American and spoiled as I could, she wiped the sweat from her eyes, took ten seconds away from her work, and smiled. She did not speak. Neither, did I. For ten seconds, our eyes met, and we smiled. I walked on towards my life and she sat there living hers.

Her face haunts me to this day. In some strange way, her smile comforts me to this day. That moment in time has defined me in a large way and is a point I go back to in my mind often. I later learned that she probably made about one dollar for a day's work of crushing rocks into gravel. That the gravel she made was used mostly for the driveways of nicer homes in the more economically sound parts of the country. That most likely, the gravel that was used on the grounds of the compound where I was staying, was made by her hands.

The first of two burdens that come with my experience of that woman on that day comes when I am tempted to complain about my situation. (I say tempted, though usually I simply complain). What right do I have to bemoan the fact that I have no cell phone service? Is it such an offense that a waiter or waitress let me sit for two minutes without filling my water glass at a meal? And yes, though I hate to admit it, if things are not going perfectly according to my notion of home or work life, should I be discontent?

The second burden comes when I get the eerie feeling that things are going too well. When I step into the kitchen and find there is drinking water running from a spigot without having to walk for miles. When I get into a vehicle and drive across town in order to eat a meal or see a friend. When my wife and family actually have enough time to consider the question, "What do you want to do?". All of these things happen without my being thankful or realizing what good fortune they are.

There is, however, a joy that comes from the elderly woman on the side of the road which I casually walked by one summer in the early nineties. It has nothing to do with material wealth or good fortune. It has nothing to do with my being more comfortable than she most likely ever was. It was her smile. It beamed. It was more memorable than most of what everyone said would be great to see in Africa. It left an impression in my soul. And the joy for me, is that each time you or I smile, we are able to create that same impression in another soul. And that, believe it or not, will be what changes the world.

Jennings Hill

Some scenes in nature are too beautiful to understand. They can only be experienced. Sunglasses, cell phones, and headphones should be avoided at all costs. Breathing should be deep, and steps should be made with intention. It was with this in mind that I found myself at the foot of Bunker Hill, the year after my mother died. The roads were not unfamiliar. We used to walk there when I was a child. The songs of different birds, the colors of the autumn leaves, the suspicion that unknown animals might be lurking in the woods, all of these brought back a rush of memories from my tumultuous raising.

Just as a ray of sunlight caught the creek I was following, I turned my head and I noticed something my years of previous hikes never included. Just up the mountain, at the end of what seemed like an overgrown path, a hint of smoke was billowing in the crisp air. These trails were known only to my family and immediately my thoughts began to focus on how I was to get this wayward camper off the property. Evening was approaching, but I had been in these woods after dark before.

As I made my way up the mountain, I wondered what my father would have done. My father was always the one that wanted to keep our part of Jennings Hill a secret. He had seen the way national parks had encouraged people from all walks of life to enjoy nature, but he had also seen the way those same people treated the land and the animals around the parks. My father never claimed to own any of the mountain, but felt the mountain owned him. This is why he always admonished me to take care of the land as if it was letting you live rent free. "Be a steward.", he would say.

Then there was my mother. She loved everyone. Everyone loved her. Every tree was a home for this or that creature and every tree provided shade for anyone that need to be sheltered. She invited people up the Hill on several occasions and for any reason. Nothing, and I mean nothing, was too much to ask of her. She was a servant of not only the land, but of people as well. Her thought, which tended to be mine as well, would have been to leave it alone. If a man or woman found enough wood to burn a fire and stay warm overnight, what harm would it do?

With my older brother miles away, living a life far removed from our mountain home, and my younger sister overdosing as a young twenty something, there was only me left to tend to the needs of our family's part of what some might call heaven. Discussions of a horseback trail and farm were thrown around after mom died. My brother even suggested we develop a resort community and predicted it would be surrounded by tourist in ten years anyway. With my parents gone, even for me, there seemed little need to keep Jennings Hill the way it was when my father's father first made it his own.

My thoughts wandered further and further into my past as I walked along what seemed at times to be a trail and at times simply overgrown forest. They also wandered into the past of the trees growing there. How many of these trees saw the Cherokee making a life in the mountains. How many shooting stars had they witnessed as the light of those stars lit up the night? What must the air have been like before Interstate 40 began to carry little carbon monoxide making machines east and west across the country? How many families of squirrels, bears, birds, and deer had they provided for? And for what reason… wait… where was I?

The evening sky had turned from a deep red to a dark blue. The sunlight had been replaced by moonbeams. And while I was accustomed to seeing in the night by moonlight, I had lost my way. Thinking too much about the way things were and are, always left me a little more than disoriented. Fear was never an issue. This hill was my own growing up. I knew every creek, cliff, and vista. What I did not recognize was what was right in front of me. It must have been the source of the smoke from earlier and seen from far below. A cabin. Not a new cabin. This cabin must have been over one hundred years old. And from inside, a light.

Not knowing who, or what, could have built this dwelling on my family's property so many years ago, I hesitated to approach. It may have been the chill in the night mountain air, or it may have been the fatigue of a full day's hike, but for whatever reason, I found myself standing on the aging but solid porch, poised to knock on the door. Fear, of what I am still unsure, now was an issue. Typically, if I had known I was going to be this deep into the woods and this far up the mountainside, I would have brought my pistol. There I stood, even unsure I had my pocket knife.

If someone lived here, they certainly would not be expecting a guest. They certainly would not think that a visitor would arrive this long after dark.

For a moment I was paralyzed. The only thing worse than knocking on the door of this cabin now, would be being discovered walking off the porch unannounced. Peeking in the window was not even an option. All there was to do was to knock and hope for the best. Perhaps the resident of this old, but well-kept cabin, would be a gracious host or hostess. So, I knocked. I knocked twice, hesitated, and knocked quickly three more times. God only knows why I remember the specific pattern of my request for warmth and rest.

The noise from inside did not seem rushed. It sounded as if a wooden chair was slid slowly across a wood floor. The sound of footsteps grew louder, along with a distinct knock with every second step. My inclination was to speak. To give some voice to my arrival. My tongue was thick, and my breath was gone. I could not muster even a grunt or sigh. The light in the room moved as if carried by the person that was either, in my mind, going to be a friend or foe.

After the sound of footsteps ceased and after the light quit moving about the room, the door moved away from me. I did not flinch. Not because I was brave or resolved to present myself as a bigger man than I was, but because nothing in my body was able to move. Soon after the door had been opened completely, I saw, in the glow of an oil lamp covered by a crude glass sleeve, a small, elderly woman. She showed signs of living and aging that I was not accustomed to seeing. Her face was grooved. Not wrinkled but grooved. Her long gray hair was braided and ran past her waist. She held the lamp to my face, and I could see her eyes squint as she said, "I was expecting you".

She turned and faced the fireplace in the one room cabin and walked back to the chair that was slid after my knocking. She sat down and placed the primitive light on the table which revealed another chair at the table (the fire for heat had nearly gone out). All this while I stood standing at the door, unable to move. Maybe out of fright or maybe out of pure astonishment, but standing at the door, none the less. She turned to me and said with a sly grin, "You missed supper. I will sleep here, you take the bed. There is firewood around back, stoke the fire and get some rest. We have a big day tomorrow. And for the love of Pete, shut the door. It will do no good to stoke the fire if you leave the door open."

After retrieving wood for the fire and building the flame, I looked behind me to the table and there this woman sat, slumped over, and snoring just a bit. I turned the wick down on the lamp and saw the antique bed with an obviously hand-made quilt covering a lumpy, down mattress, with some measure of guilt, settled in for the night. Before sleep found me, I wondered what in the world was happening. Who was this woman? How did I end up here? How had I not known about her before? And what in the world could she have meant when she said she was expecting me?

When I woke the next morning, I wondered what brew I had been drinking the night before to have such vivid and strange dreams. Dreaming for me was easy in those days and I remembered being in odd situations before in my sleep, but an old woman on Jennings Hill expecting me in the middle of the night topped them all. This dream was the craziest one of all, except for this, it was not a dream at all. Startled a little by her stare, I was finally able to speak and said, "Thank you so much for your kindness".

She grinned and revealed several gaps in her mouth where teeth might have been in earlier years and said, "It is good to have company. It has been so long since you have visited".

Almost in protest, I said "Ma'am, this is the first time I have been in this place".

This elderly woman was most certainly insane. Somehow, the mountain life in solitude had driven her to the brink of insanity. But really, who was I to speak on such matters. I was still unsure as to my mental state and if I was on some bad trip, from some drug, I had ingested in my college years. The moments after our initial words were awkward. She just stared at me with some silly, but somehow knowing, grin. My eyes scanned the cabin with a quick dart to determine her disposition from time to time. She finally spoke again and said, "My name is Joanna. And, of course, you are Johnathan Jennings".

Immediately I reached around to my back pocket to confirm my billfold was still in my possession. Joanna could not have known who I was without picking through my billfold. It was in my pocket. My mind raced and at that instant, I wanted to run out of the cabin and take my chances on getting as far away from this woman, that would not quit smiling, as I could. She reached behind her to the rustic shelving attached to the cabin wall and produced some nuts and berries. She motioned me to the table as she sat in one of the chairs.

"How did you sleep?", Joanna said.

After some thought, I said, "Better than I have in a long time".

"You were tired", she said.

We shared the food she had provided and spoke for some time about small things. Things two people who had just met might discuss, but

different. There was no talk of "what do you do?",
and "where do you work?". There was no
conversation about "where did you get your car?" or
"what part of town do you live in?". We spoke
mostly about my journey to her cabin and briefly
about how she slept the night before hunched over
in a dinner chair. After a while, I could not hold the
question any longer and asked, "How did you know
to expect me? Was it a vision? Did you see me
coming from your vantage point?"

Joanna smiled a simple smile and gently
said, "Johnathan, in my many years on this earth, I
have learned to expect good things. And, you son,
are a good thing".

I melted in the chair. No one had ever said
this to me. My mind immediately wanted to know
what the angle was. What could she possibly want?
It was a little uncomfortable but at the same time as
if my heart was hearing life's words for the first
time. What could I do with a statement like that? If I
say thank you, she might think, that I think, I am
actually a good thing. If I disagreed, she might think

I am faking humility. What, when you really think about it, do you do with someone saying, simply, "you are a good thing"?

It was easy to see by the light of the sun and the shadow it cast, that it was time for me to make my way back down the mountain to my life. Sundays were usually slow, but always had a hint of sadness, as I would have to travel back to the city to spend a week working on this or that project for my boss. If I was to make it to work on time, which I always struggled with, I would have to leave soon. I rose from the table and bowed a little and said, "Joanna, it was great meeting you. Thank you so much for allowing me to stay the night and for the breakfast, but it is time for me to go. For what it is worth, I do not mind that you are on my family's land. You must have been here a long time without trouble, and you are welcome to stay as long as you like."

Joanna laughed. She laughed loud, long, and hard. She got up from the table and walked slowly towards me, put her frail arms around my neck, gave me a hug as firm as she could, and said, "Thank you for your kindness, Johnathan".

She stepped back and asked me a question. "Would you let me share something with you for your allowing me to stay on this land in my cabin? I do not have much, so it will be some bits of wisdom you might take with you."

Reluctantly, I said yes. What could Joanna know more than me? She obviously is poor. She has no friends that I could tell. She has no running water and the only productive thing she might have done in the last years is allow me to stay the night in comfort. But, even still, I said, yes.

She sat back in one of the two chairs and invited me to do the same. She looked into my eyes and began to speak.

"Always see something different in the routines of life. Realize that you are not the same person you were the day before. Realize that others are not the same people they were yesterday, either. Take the good from your thoughts and make more good thoughts. Let the worry and stress of the day fend for itself as you see only the possibilities in people for goodness. Only the possibilities of better things for the world and for a real and lasting peace among those who live in it."

Know in your heart there is a God. Know also that you will not know its name or know it fully. Although this is true, be sure of the fact that it knows you and wants only good for you. When faced with a choice between being right or being happy, choose happiness every time. When faced with a challenge you cannot face alone, ask for help, from others and from the Divine. You are not alone.

Make time for silence. Make time for song. Make time for times when time is not a reality. And if you must, make time for generating more wealth. The root of all evil is not the love of money. The root of evil is the love of more money. Let the first thing you say be 'thank you' and the last thing before you sleep be peace. Do not let the gifts of God keep you from seeking the will of God.

Remember you are good but remember also that you are not so important. Power over anything in this world comes with an intoxication that clouds the decisions of the weak. Live for others and you will find yourself. There is more goodness that comes from a simple act of kindness than the command of wealth or men. Be gracious.

Laugh. Laugh at the world. Laugh at bad jokes. Laugh, most of all, at and with yourself. There are two things you cannot do and worry at the same time. You cannot laugh and be worried. You cannot be grateful and worry. Practice both regularly. Laughter and gratitude.

And lastly, the thing I would like for you to do most, is come see your grandmother again."

My jaw dropped. It all came rushing back to me. These roads were familiar because they were traveled with much smaller legs. This cabin was familiar because my toddler summers were spent on this woman's knee. I asked Joanna, my grandmother, how it was that she had come to live here by herself and how she had not continued to be

a part of my life. She and my mother had fought
years ago. And as ridiculous as it was, the hike up
the mountain became less important for my parents.

My grandmother said she had heard about
my sister and keeps up with my brother and me on
social media… what? What do you know about
social media and how do you have access to such
things? "Johnathan", she said, I live in a cabin in the
woods on a hillside. Not because I have to, but
because I choose to. When I sold this land to your
mother and father, this is all I wanted. Quite
frankly, I am rich beyond your wildest imaginings
and a satellite-based cell phone is a very minor
expense".

For the second time that day, my jaw
dropped. In the following years, my wife and three
children made it to the cabin on Jennings Hill twice
a month without fail. When my grandmother passed
into the heavens, she was alone. I say alone. She
was without a physical companion. We found her
slumped over her table with a lamp that had since
run out of oil. Next to the lamp was a paper with

words written with ink and a shaky hand, that read,
"I have lived my life without regret. There are better things waiting for me. It is now for you only to smile when you think of me".

This is what I do from time to time, amidst my busy life. I smile. Not only because I think of her, but because in some ways, it keeps her present in the world. And that smile is what the world needs. I still find myself laughing for no reason and being grateful for everything that comes my way.

You Are a Big Deal

Everyone has heard advice in their lives. Everyone, from the time they came into human form, has heard what it is they must do. There is no manual. For the most part, those giving advice are guessing, based on what is important to them. If you were lucky, you heard advice that compelled you to grow into a wonderful, well put together, at peace, caring, compassionate, thinking, independent, content, human being. But, really, is not this assessment just a back handed way of my offering advice on what you should be?

Think what you will of me, but I will share a story from my career as a youth worker in a Methodist church, which in some ways, tells a tale of me, and in some ways, shows my inexperience at the time.

Our group went to a conference in a local tourist town. We found ourselves in a service with around 1500 other attendees, in what the Methodists wanted to believe, was a cool, hip, meeting, that would show kids how relevant Jesus was, even years after his death. Beside me was Joanna, a student in eighth grade, who was shy, but cool. Awkward, but most likely destined to be a great student, in a great school, with plenty of friends. Behind me, was Joanna's mother, who never cared much for me or my style of teaching.

After the music was over, the speaker ran out of breath, and the light show died down, there was a traditional eucharist (Christians use this to celebrate the Last Supper of Christ), which was administered by the method of intinction (participants take bread, dip it in a communal cup of wine, and consume the bread). This was all new to me, as I had not experienced this method of what I commonly call, "The Lord's Supper". Joanna turned to me and said, "I am not sure if I should do this", to which I replied, "It is up to you".

Joanna said, "My mom thinks it's nasty".

I said, "It is up to you".

After the service, Joanna's mother unleashed all the furies of what could be described as, all three hells, on me as we retrieved the vans to pick the group up and haul them back home. After she explained the virtues of my doing only what she, as a parent, wanted me to do, with regard to her child, she looked at me with a dignified rage and said, "Don't you ever, ever, tell my child to do something I have told her not to do!".

To which I replied, "Peggy… Jesus is going to do that someday".

Now that I am a parent, I understand her frustration. Now that I have listened to Creator a little more in life, I understand my point, as well. To me, it has become an amusing antidote in the story of my life. I am unsure what became of Joanna and Peggy. Peggy's attempts to have me removed from my position failed, but eventually I determined there were easier ways to affect lives than by being paid by an organized religion. "Jah Love" to all those that work in those conditions.

None the less, here all three of us were, with three different experiences of the same conference. All three of us in different placcs in our growth and maturity. All three of us with different opinions of what we were entitled to know and say. When I think back on that day, and those days, I smile still. Mostly at how important I thought I was and how important Peggy thought she was. Usually, when I consult the Divine on the matter, I hear the Divine giggle a little at how important I thought I was. I recognize the laughter because I hear it still when I take all my pressing, urgent concerns to the Universe for solutions.

What in the world would this story have to do with you? Why is this shared when the title suggested that YOU are a big deal. You are a big deal. Not for what religion you adhere to. Not for what you think you know of the Creator. Not because of your job, your clothes, your reputation, how many times your Little League team won state titles, your GPA in high school, or how well you adhered to the direct commands of your parents. Not for what you did yesterday or for what you plan to do tomorrow. You are the perfect manifestation of what the Creator of the universe thought the world needed in the instant you were created.

Sometimes we interpret "work in progress" as a negative thing. We hear the word, "work", and do not focus on the word, "progress". We are in transition. If you do not believe me, think of what you believed ten years ago and ask yourself if those beliefs have changed. Find a photograph of yourself ten years ago and compare it to what is reflected in any nearby mirror. We are changing, even if we do not intend to change, simply by the fact that the world is changing, and we are still able to navigate our way through the world. And this, my friends, is progress. It is growth.

Growth is not the fact that we have a better job, or more friends, or that we drive a newer car. Growth is not a better credit rating. Growth is what we have shared. Not money, but what is measured by how much of what the Divine has given us, that has been shared with others. We do not need participation trophies for every competition, but perhaps we need less competitions. What if we measured growth by the success of those around us? What if we did not feel the need to measure growth at all?

Personally, I prefer to remember moments of contentment more than I enjoy remembering anything I have accomplished, or any game I have won. The secret for me, is that contentment can be generated at any time, in any circumstance. It is always a possibility. Accomplishments, or wins, are good. But they cannot be created "on demand".

You are a big deal. A really, really, big deal.

About that notion that the Divine is laughing. I promise you it happens more than you think. Never in a meanspirited way. Always in Love. The laughter is a result of the Universe knowing how limited our minds are when we try to find solutions. How troubled we are by things beyond our control. And, yes, how important we think we are. You are a big deal if you can learn to laugh with the Creator, but, regardless, you are a big enough deal for the Creator to seek you, to find you where you are and how you are, and to teach you to turn your tears into, at the least, a slight grin, caused by the suspicion, that where you are now, is not where you will be tomorrow. You are not a "work in progress", but Baby Girl, Little Man, you ARE progress.

There are a lot of big deals in this world. For my son Carter and me, helping others help others is one of them. We have created Compassion Waves Card Company in an effort to spread joy and help homeless and low-income individuals generate income. We sell cards and apparel. We allow homeless and lower income people to resell our products. We are excited about our website, CompassionWaves.com going "live".

Our thought idea was based on a documentary seen on Netflix about social capitalism, called "A New Capitalism". There is a quote by Andre Albuquerque, of Fundador Do Terra Nova, in the film that conveys the thought, "If eliminating poverty was done simply out of brotherly love, it might take 5,000 years, but if eliminating poverty were good business for everyone, it might only take 500 years".

We have all, most likely, heard the saying, "Give a man to fish, and feed him for a day. Teach a man to fish and feed him for a lifetime". I would add, "Teach a kid to teach a man to fish and change the world".